FORESTS AND TREES

OF

KARNATAKA

A JOURNEY IN TIME
THROUGH BUCHANAN'S EYES

DIPAK SARMAH, IFS (Retd.)

Formerly PCCF (HoFF), PCCF, Wildlife,

Secretary (Forest), Government of Karnataka

INDIA · SINGAPORE · MALAYSIA

Notion Press Media Pvt Ltd

No. 50, Chettiyar Agaram Main Road,
Vanagaram, Chennai, Tamil Nadu – 600 095

First Published by Notion Press 2021
Copyright © Dipak Sarmah, IFS (Retd.) 2021
All Rights Reserved.

ISBN 978-1-63940-340-0

*This book is dedicated to the fond memory of Shri S. Shyam Sunder,
IFS (Retd.), the evergreen forester, who is no more, but is always with us.*

– Dipak Sarmah

BOOKS FROM THE AUTHOR

Status of Forests of Karnataka (2018)

Forestry in Karnataka – A Journey of 150 Years (2019)

Forests of Karnataka – A Panoramic View (2019)

Wildlife Management in Karnataka – A Forester's Perspective (2019)

Forestry in India during British Era – Karnataka Case-Study (2020)

Agroforestry in Karnataka – A Golden Opportunity for Green Growth (2020)

Dry Deciduous Forests of Karnataka – Adding Years to Their Life, and to Ours (2021)

Author's Contact Details:

Dipak Sarmah

245, NTI Layout, 8th Main

Vidyaranyapura, Bengaluru – 560 097

Mob: 9986232094

e-mail: sarmahdipak1@gmail.com

CONTENTS

PREFACE

The beginning of the 19th century was a significant phase in the history of the State of Karnataka. In 1800, after the defeat and death of Tipu Sultan in the Fourth Anglo-Mysore War (1799), the princely State of Mysore came into being under the oversight of the British East India Company. Earlier, during the Third Anglo-Mysore War (1790-1792), the Company had wrested Canara, and then Malabar, from Tipu. Having gained control over vast territories comprising Mysore, Malabar and Canara, the British were keen to know all about the newly-acquired areas. With this objective in mind, the then Governor-General of India, Lord Wellesley, without any loss of time, instructed Dr. Francis Buchanan to travel through and report upon the newly conquered territories. Dr. Buchanan was a Scottish surgeon in the East India Company's Service in the Bengal medical establishment. He was a man reputed to have been 'gifted with a mind well-fitted for acute observation and also equipped with the requisite scientific and technical knowledge'. Although a surgeon by profession, Dr. Buchanan was also a botanist, zoologist, geographer and surveyor. In compliance with the orders of the Government, Dr. Buchanan had undertaken a long journey through Mysore, Malabar and Canara during 1800 and 1801. He had set out from Madras on the 23rd of April, 1800 and returned to Madras on the 6th of July, 1801. Buchanan wrote his report day by day, while travelling, in the form of a journal. The Directors of the East India Company in receiving it were so pleased that they ordered its publication. It accordingly made its appearance, in three volumes, in 1807, styled '*A Journey from Madras through the Countries of Mysore, Canara and Malabar*'. Although Buchanan had wished to abridge the book and alter its arrangement before its publication, he could not undertake such alterations, as the printing had commenced before his arrival in England in 1806 and as his stay in England was for a brief period. The book covers various aspects such as topography, history, antiquities, the condition of the inhabitants, religion, natural resources (particularly forests, mines, quarries, and fisheries,), agriculture (covering crops, fruits and vegetables, implements, manure, floods, domestic animals, fences, farms, and landed property), revenue administration, fine and common arts, and commerce (exports and imports, weights and measures, currencies, and conveyance of goods). Being a very keen observer, he had given vivid, and at times amusing, description of the traits of the various people he had come across during the course of his long journey. Buchanan's book provides fairly good account of the administrative, economic, social and cultural systems obtaining in Mysore, Malabar and Canara during the early 1800s.

Buchanan's travel-diaries became an important source of information for the rulers who, having acquired vast knowledge about an immensely diverse region in such a short span of time, were in a position to more effectively administer the newly-acquired areas and their inhabitants. These travel-diaries have proved to be equally helpful to historians and others also, as they provide a fairly authentic and impartial glimpse of the general condition of the country covering various aspects such as the terrain, climate, soil, agriculture, manufacture, industry, economy, trade and commerce, people, occupations, lifestyles, social customs, religions, art, culture, etc. pertaining to the period during Tipu Sultan's administration and immediately thereafter. 'The luminous report containing the result of the investigations made by Dr. Francis Buchanan in 1800 and 1801 is the main source of information for the purpose mentioned.' [Modern Mysore (1936)]

Buchanan was an accomplished botanist with a lot of passion for exploring the plant world. However, he had not undertaken the long journey through Mysore, Malabar and Canara for botanical exploration. His main objective was to know about the country and her people and to submit a comprehensive report to the Government. But the botanist in him was always alive and kicking throughout the journey. As he travelled along the pre-determined route through various regions of Mysore and

Canara, he noted the changes in the landscape in terms of vegetation and its composition. On a few occasions, when he had passed through forests, he got specimens of the trees collected, discussed with the local people about their uses etc. and described in his diaries. A large part of his journey was through inhabited areas which enabled him to know extensively about different crops and agricultural practices and also about the people inhabiting the villages. In these areas too, Buchanan made it a point to note the fruit and other trees grown on the farmlands; more particularly, he noted the trees/plants used for manure, as hedge plants, as nurse crop, and for supporting vines. His interest in botany was so deep that, while travelling around Periyapatna, he did not fail to notice the rank weeds such as *Ocymum molle*, *Datura metel*, *Amaranthus spionosus*, *Mirabilis jalappa*, *Tagetes erecta*, etc. which had come up spontaneously 'near the villages, where the ground is manured by the soil of the inhabitants, and of their cattle.'

Buchanan had devoted considerable time of his travel at the important trading centers where, besides ascertaining the market trends, he had interacted with merchants and other people having knowledge about processing or manufacture of the commodities. As a large number of goods that were traded those days were sourced from trees or plants from the wild, Buchanan's attention was naturally drawn towards these trees or plants about which he made investigations and wrote in his diaries. Buchanan had also found that a number of important economic and industrial activities depended in one way or another on trees and other plants. These have been described by Buchanan with minute detail based on his observations as well as on the outcome of his interactions with knowledgeable people.

Buchanan's penchant for exploring the nature can be gauged from the fact that, when he was forced to overstay at Hiriyur owing to sickness of a few of his accompanying staff, he had commented thus: "All objects of enquiry having been soon exhausted, while the desert nature of the country precluded any resource from botany, my stay at *Heriuru* became very tedious." But Buchanan did not remain idle; he went to the nearby stream called *Vedawati* to cool himself and returned with a catch of three species of *Cyprinus* (fish) and presented their detailed, almost photo-like, drawings in his diaries.

The book *Forests and Trees of Karnataka - A Journey in Time through Buchanan's Eyes* attempts at providing a pen picture of the forests and trees of Karnataka as seen by Buchanan during his journey undertaken in 1800 and 1801. As Buchanan's narrations contained in the three volumes of his journal cover a very wide range of subjects, his observations specifically on trees and plants have been culled out and presented in the form of a book. Based on Buchanan's observations, an attempt has been made at visualizing the forest scenario of Karnataka more than 200 years ago. The book also highlights the important role trees and plants were assigned in the distant past to complement agricultural operations and industrial activities leading to economic development and general welfare. In the book, Buchanan's narrations have been mostly reproduced verbatim not only to retain the flavor of the language and the authenticity of the content but also in reverence to Buchanan's enviable adroitness in the economy in use of words.

– DIPAK SARMAH

Chapter 1

INTRODUCTION

Dr. Francis Buchanan belonged to a period when forest was viewed purely as an economic resource. A forest was considered valuable on the basis of the value of its constituents. A forest harboring teak or sandal trees was considered to be a prized asset. A forest containing other hardwood trees was also considered useful but relatively less valuable. Forest harboring softwood trees was thought to be dispensable, being of no use. However, by and large, all trees that were known to be of some utility on account of any of their parts including leaves, flowers, fruits, seed, bark, etc. were also considered valuable, and were therefore preserved or nurtured. During that period, forest did not have any intrinsic right over land. Agriculture was given primacy and forest was assigned a subservient role to promote or complement agriculture. Whenever any forest land was considered fit for cultivation or was required for any other purpose, it was sacrificed without a second thought. The idea that a forest, irrespective of its economic importance, had an overarching ecological role to play for the overall wellbeing of the people had not yet evolved. [**Note:** The beneficial role of forest in terms of its ecological services came to be appreciated in the latter years, sometime during the 1850s, when persons like Dr. Hugh Cleghorn and Dr. Alexander Gibson, again from the medical fraternity, appeared in the forestry scene of India, as if to heal the forests.]

Mysore Kingdom was known for its sandalwood resources since a very long time. The best sandal growing areas of the kingdom came to the Mysore State's share. There was some sandalwood in the Company's territories of Canara and Kollegal also. Since sandalwood was a very important source of revenue for the Government, Buchanan had taken a lot of interest in knowing about the species during his travel. In his diaries, Buchanan provided fairly detailed account regarding sandal as he came across the tree a number of times during the course of his long journey. He had also gathered valuable information about the tree and its wood from knowledgeable people with whom he had interactions during his journey. A good deal of information about the occurrence of sandal and its ecology, and about the status of trade of sandalwood during that period can be elicited from Buchanan's diaries. These are discussed in the following chapter (*Chapter 2*).

Peninsular India was also very famous for teak trees. Teak trees of Canara, Mysore (HD Kote) and Shimoga were exploited even during the times of Haider Ali and Tipu Sultan. The British had a special interest in teak as they were in need of high quality teak logs for the Royal Navy of the Kingdom of Great Britain. Even otherwise, there was good demand for teak as a construction timber within India also. It was therefore quite natural for Buchanan to ascertain the occurrence and abundance of teak trees in different parts of the country that he passed through. His observations on the availability and growth of teak have been dealt in a separate chapter (*Chapter 3*).

During his travel, Buchanan came across forests harboring bamboo a number of times. Having seen the forests of the eastern part of India (Bengal and Chittagong), Buchanan was quite aware of the benefits that people can derive from bamboos. This must be one of the reasons as to why Buchanan showed interest regarding the occurrence of bamboo and its utilization by the people of Mysore and Canara. His descriptions about bamboo have been brought out separately in *Chapter 4*.

Buchanan had also noticed that in addition to sandal and teak, there were many other trees in the forest that were economically important and a number of commodities traded in the market were sourced from such trees. This naturally led Buchanan to delve further into the art and science of how the raw materials were collected and processed leading to the final products. His narrations provide a broad overview of the society's dependence on the bounties of the Mother Nature including a wide range of items such as gum, oil, leaves, flowers, fruits, seeds, bark, roots, tubers, insects, etc., besides timber and fuel wood. These have been discussed in *Chapter 5*.

Buchanan had spent a considerable part of his travel time in learning about the agricultural crops and agricultural operations. As the crops as well as the operations varied from region to region, he diligently took note of the differences and described them in his diaries. During those days, people were aware of the intrinsic relationship between agricultural operations and trees or other plants. Trees, shrubs and herbs were extensively used for various purposes including retention of moisture, improvement of soil fertility, crop protection, etc. Buchanan had closely observed the different trees, shrubs and herbs used for these purposes in different regions and described these in detail in his diaries. He had also given detailed account about gardens and orchards that he came across in various parts of the country. These have been discussed in *Chapter 6* and *Chapter 7*, respectively.

As already mentioned in the preface, trees and other plants contributed to the country's economic and industrial activities in a number of ways. Activities such as smelting of iron, manufacture of steel, textile manufacture, leather works, distillation, processing of agricultural products, etc. depended upon trees and other plants not only as the primary source of energy in the form of fuel wood or charcoal, but also as secondary or feeder items that were used to facilitate or accelerate the activities. These have been described by Buchanan with minute detail based on his observations as well as on his interactions with knowledgeable people. These have been discussed in *Chapter 8*.

Although Buchanan passed through forest areas on a number of occasions, he described the constituent trees in some detail only on four occasions. In Mysore State, he came across more agricultural lands (including abandoned lands) than forest lands, as he travelled along roads that mainly passed through habitations. However, Buchanan quite often gave his general impression about the countryside, its natural vegetation and constituent trees or plants. In addition, his observations regarding mining and smelting of iron ore, tiger menace, fuel wood availability, etc. throw some light on the general status of forest of the country during the distant past. These and related matters are discussed in two chapters: in *Chapter 9* for Mysore State, and in *Chapter 10*, for Canara.

ROUTE TAKEN BY BUCHANAN

In order to appreciate the vastness of the geographical area that Buchanan had covered in Mysore and Canara, it may be relevant to have an idea about the route that he had taken during his long journey. As already mentioned, Buchanan had set out from Madras on 23rd April, 1800. He was travelling mostly on bullock-cart. After travelling through Poonamalai, Sri Perambathur, Conjeevaram, Wallajapet, Arcot, Vellore and Venkatagiri, Buchanan entered the Mysore State, reaching Bethamangala (*Byadamungulum*) on 5th May, 1800. Thereafter, he travelled through Tekal (*Tayculum*), Malur (*Waluru*), Kadugodi (*Catcolli*), and reached Bangalore on the morning of 10th May, 1800. He halted at Bangalore for two days and proceeded further via Kengeri, Bidadi, Channapatna, Maddur, and Mandya, reaching Srirangapatna on 17th May. On 18th May, 1800, he delivered his credentials and was formally employed by the Government. He had an interview with *Purnea*, the *Dewan* of Mysore, on the next day. From 20th May to 5th June, Buchanan stayed at Srirangapatna, visiting various parts of the town and its neighbourhood, taking account of diverse subjects including administration, the city and its buildings, population, state of agriculture, livestock, commerce, manufactures, currency, weights and measures, etc.

Buchanan made three trips from Srirangapatna and travelled to various parts of Mysore State and the East India Company's territories of Kollegal, Malabar and Canara. The first trip commenced on 5th June, 1800, when Buchanan travelled to Ramanagara, Magadi, Tavarekere, Bangalore (second time), Malur, Vokkaleri, Kolar, *Calura*, Sidlaghatta, Chikkaballapur, Doddaballapur, Madhugiri, Sira, Tumkur, Gubbi, Chikkanayakanahalli, Turuvekere, Bellur, Nagamangala and Melkote, finally returning to Srirangapatna on 1st September, 1800. The second trip started on 5th September, 1800, when Buchanan travelled to Palhalli, Periyapatna, Heggadadevankote, Hampapura, Nanjangud, Mysore, T. Narasipura, and Malingy. On 3rd October, Buchanan left Malingy, crossed the Mysore territory, and entered the Company's territory at Kollegal where he travelled through Kollegal, Sattegal, Sivanasamudra, Barachukki, Gaganachukki, Singanalluru, Hanur, Cowdalli and Martahalli and then, on 10th October, 1800, proceeded to Malabar via Coimbatore. After completing his tour of Malabar, Buchanan entered Canara and reached Mangalore on 22nd January, 1801. He camped at Mangalore up to 29th January, 1801, and then toured the southern parts of Canara covering the places such as Bantwal, Belthangady, Jamalabad, Moodabidri, Karkala, Udupi, Brahmavara, Kundapur, and Baindur. From 18th February, he travelled through the northern parts of Canara and visited the places including Bhatkal, Shirali, Bailur, Honnavar, Haldipur, Kumta, Mirjan, Hiregutti, Gokarna, Ankola, Chandya, Belekeri, Karwar, Sadashivagad, Gopshitta, Kadra, Avila-gotna, Devakar, *Barabuli* (Baravalli), *Cutaki* (Kattige), Yellapura, Sonda, Sirsi, and Banavasi. On 18th March, 1801, Buchanan entered the Mysore State at Chandragutti in present Shivamogga district. From here, he travelled through Keladi, Ikkeri, Sagara, Nagara, Kaval durga, Hodalla (near Thirthahalli), Mahishi, Tudur, Mandagadde, Shimoga, Kudali, Sasvehalli, Basavapatna, Harihar, Davanagere, Chitradurga, Hiriyur, Yelladakere, Hosadurga, Budhihal, Garudanagiri, Banavara, Javagal, Halebeedu, Belur, Halthore, Hassan, Channarayapatna, and Shravanabelagola, and returned to Srirangapatna. In his final trip, Buchanan left Srirangapatna on 4th June, 1801, and visited Bannur, Sosale, Malavalli, Halaguru, Sathnur, Kanakanahalli (Kanakapura) and Maralawadi which was the last place he visited in the Mysore territory and from here he entered the Company's territory (June 14, 1801) and proceeded towards Madras via Thalli, Denkanikottai, Krishnagiri, Tirupathur, Vaniambadi, Amboor, Vellore, Wallajapet and other places, reaching Madras on 6th July, 1801.

Chapter 2

SANDALWOOD IN MYSORE AND CANARA

During the period when Buchanan had visited the Mysore State, sandalwood was one of the most important products of the State. Sandal trees occurred not only in forest areas but also in and around farmlands and habitations. As a result, Buchanan came across the tree at a number of places during the course of his journey. Being an accomplished botanist and also keeping in mind the enormous potential of this tree in generating revenue for the State, Buchanan had made detailed enquiries regarding all aspects of the tree and its prized wood. His diaries are replete with his incisive observations.

Interestingly, Buchanan came across sandal trees soon after entering the Mysore State. During his travel from Madras to Srirangapatna, Buchanan saw sandal trees on 7th May, 1800, when he was passing through the present Kolar district. In Malur (mentioned by Buchanan as *Waluru*) he had visited a castle then occupied by a *Rajput* and his family comprising fifteen members. The ancestors of this man were formerly *Jagirdars* of the place and of villages in the neighbourhood. The outer wall of the castle had a strong hedge of seegekai (*Acacia concinna*) climbers and sandal trees, which Buchanan described as follows:

'Shicai, **or** *Mimosa saponaria* **and Sandal-wood**. – The outer wall is surrounded by a strong hedge of the *Mimosa saponaria;* the fruit of which, called *Shicai,* is used as soap for washing the hair. The leaves, which are acid, serve the poor instead of tamarinds, which are much used in the cookery of the southern *Hindus.* The hedge is rented at *20 Pagodas* (*6£. 4s. 7d.*) a year; for the fruit is an article of trade, that is carried even so far as *Madras,* where three pods are said to cost 1 *dub,* or small *pice.* In the same hedge about twenty years ago were planted some *Sandal-wood* trees, which, although surrounded by the *Mimosa,* a strong scandent shrub, seem to be healthy; but, as none of them have yet been cut down, it is impossible to ascertain how far they will be valuable."

On his way from Bangalore to Srirangapatna, Buchanan had camped at Bidadi (then known as *Wiridy* or *Biridy*) for a day (May 13, 1800). During his evening walk in the nearby woods, Buchanan was shown a number of trees as being useful. These included the sandal tree also. Buchanan described the tree as follows:

"*Sri Gunda Chica, Santalum album,* Lin. Grows in the woods towards *Chinapatam.* It is never planted, but springs up spontaneously. No person is allowed to cut it, without permission from the *Amildar,* or officer, who sells it on account of the *Circar,* or government."

During the above walk, Buchanan gathered the information that the bark of the sandal tree was also used as a substitute for betel-nut (areca nut).

In the course of his journey from Srirangapatna to Bangalore (second visit), Buchanan had passed through the forests of *Savana-durga* in Magadi (June 15-19, 1800). He gave a very detailed account of a large number of tree species found in the forests and their important uses. The tree specimens were brought to him by the local woodmen for examination. With regard to the sandal tree, Buchanan made the following observations which throw some light on the growth characteristics of the tree and the method of extraction as well as dressing of sandalwood as were prevalent during that period.

"*Sri Gunda, Santalum album. Sandal-wood* of the English merchants. All the trees that were fit for sale have been lately cut by a *Brahman*, who was sent on purpose from *Seringapatam*. He procured about three thousand trees; but in less than ten years no more will be fit for cutting. The common size of the tree at the root, when it is cut, is about nine inches in diameter; but it has been known to arrive at a circumference of three cubits. In either case, not above a third of the diameter of the tree is of value; the remainder is white wood, totally devoid of smell. The wood is of the best quality in trees that have grown on a steep rocky soil; that which grows in low rich situations produces wood of little value. The trees were cut partly by the servants of the *Brahman*, and partly by woodmen hired on the spot. The branches and white wood were removed in the woods, and the billets were brought hither, and dried in the shade. Although the bottom of the stem, under the ground and immediately above the division into roots, is the most valuable part of the tree, no pains were taken to procure this, and the trees were cut above the surface of the soil. This want of economy is said to have proceeded from the stony nature of the soil; but this I doubt. Every thing relative to the price, market, or customs upon *sandal-wood* are here unknown; and the person who cut it was not under the authority of the *Amildar*. At two places in this hilly country the tree comes to great perfection; namely, at *Jalamangala*, between *Magadi* and *Chinapatam;* and at *Mutati Habigay*, near *Capala-durga.*"

[**Note:** One cubit is equal to about 1½ feet or 18 inches.]

During his stay at Bangalore from 22nd June to 2nd July, 1800, Buchanan had met with the merchants trading in various goods and ascertained the prices of the principal articles of commerce. As regards sandalwood, the average price current at Bangalore was as indicated in the following table.

Kind of goods.	Quality.	Sultany Fanams.		English money. Cwt. £. s. d.
		Maund.	Cwt.	
Sandal-wood	Nagara 1st sort	12	52 1/8	1 15 1
	Nagara 2nd sort	10	43 4/10	1 9 2
	Nagara 3rd sort	8	34 ¾	1 3 4
	Walagram 1st sort	8	34 ¾	1 3 4
	Walagram 2nd sort	6	26 1/10	0 17 6½
	Walagram 3rd sort	5	21 9/10	0 14 7

(**Note**: One *Maund* is equal to *42½ Seers*)

Regarding the occurrence of sandal trees and the quality classes in which sandalwood was sorted, Buchanan provided the following information.

"*Sandal-wood* is also a considerable article of commerce at *Bangalore*. The best comes from the *Nagara* district, and from the country bordering on the western *Ghats*. An inferior kind comes from *Madura, Denkina-cotay, Deva-rayana-cotay*, and other places in the ridge of hills which run north from *Capala-durga*. Each kind is divided into three sorts: the first is that which is between the root and the first branches; the second is that of the large branches; and the third is that of the small branches, so far as these contain red wood. The *sandal* tree, according to the idea of the natives, is of two kinds; male and female: the former of which is dark; and the latter pale-coloured; both are of the same value. The *sandal* of the old tree is said to be more valuable than that from a young one; but the merchants, in forming an estimate of its value, go entirely by the strength of its smell. During *Tippoo's* government none of the *sandal-wood* came to this market: he either did not allow it to be cut, or else stored up in his forts whatever was felled."

While travelling through Madhugiri (July 25, 1800), Buchanan had come across many sandal trees but these were of poor quality.

"In this district, there are many sandal wood trees; but of so bad a quality, that they are never cut."

While camping at Periyapatna (September 11-13, 1800) Buchanan collected detailed information about various trees in the forests, trading practices of different forest products, etc. With regard to the sandal tree, Buchanan provided the following information covering its growth, and production, trade and smuggling of its wood.

"**Sandal-wood, *Santalum album*.** - Sandal-wood grows in the skirts of the forest. The people of *Coorg* were in the habit of stealing a great part of it; but since the country received the Company's protection they have desisted from this insolence. It is often planted in gardens and hedges; and, from the richness of the soil, grows there to a large size; but in such places the timber has little smell, and is of no value. It is a *Daray*, or stony soil only, that produces fine sandal. It may be felled at any season; and once in twelve years, whatever has grown to a proper size is generally cut. On these occasions, the district produces about 10,000 *Maunds*, or above 2000 hundred-weight. The whole was lately sold to the agents of the Bombay government, and a relation of *Purnea's* was employed to deliver it. Much to the credit of the *Dewan*, this person was put in confinement, having been detected in selling to private traders some of what he cut, and also in having sold great quantities that were found buried. During the *Sultan's* government a great deal of it arrived at maturity, which he would not sell. In general, this was privately cut, and concealed under ground, till an opportunity offered of smuggling it into the *Vir Raya's* dominions. The *Amildars* have now received orders to cut all the sandal-wood in their respective districts and to deliver it to the Bombay agents. They know nothing of the conditions of sale. At present, no sandal-oil is made at *Priya-pattana.*"

It is interesting to note that more than two hundred years ago, Buchanan, based on his limited observations, very precisely and adequately commented upon the growth and ecology of the sandal tree. He had also brought out the darker side of the then administration (Purnea's favoritism to his relative or community) as also the brighter side of the administration (Purnea's sense of administration of justice). Buchanan had also highlighted the basic ills of administration such as corruption and smuggling.

During his tour through HD Kote (September 19, 1800), Buchanan collected a lot of information about sandal trees grown in the region as well as in the adjoining Coorg region, and also about the extraction, processing, trade, etc. of sandalwood. Based on these, Buchanan made the following very elaborate observations and comments.

"**Sandal-wood. *Santalum album***. - *Hegodu Devana Cotay* is one of the most considerable districts for the produce of sandal-wood; and I found there a Portuguese agent of the Commercial Resident at *Mangalore*, who was employed to collect a purchase of this article that had been made by the government of Bombay from the *Dewan* of *Mysore*. Two thousand *Candies*, each weighing 520 lb. were to have been delivered at a stipulated period; but this has not been fulfilled. Orders, indeed, have long ago been issued to the *Amildars* for accomplishing it; but a prompt execution of any such commands is by no means usual in an Indian government. The account which this agent gave is as follows: the *Amildars*, having no legal profit for this extraordinary trouble, endeavour to squeeze something out of the workmen. They charge the wages given to these poor people at ¼ of a *Fanam* a day, which is the usual rate of the country; and, in place of this, give them only half a *Seer* of *Ragy*. The labourers, being thus forced to work at a low allowance, throw in his way every obstacle in their power. It is the lowest and most ignorant of the peasantry, in place of tradesmen, that have been selected. A sufficient number having been seized, they are ordered each to bring a billet of sandal to the *Cutchery*, or office of the *Amildar*. Every man immediately seizes on the tree nearest him; cuts it down, whether it be ripe or not; neglects the part nearest the root, as being more troublesome to get at, and drags the tree to the appointed place, after having taken off the bark to render it lighter. Before the office the logs lie exposed to sun, wind, and rain, until other peasants, as ignorant as the former, can be pressed to cut off the white wood with their miserable hatchets. These cut the billets of all lengths, according as every man thinks it will be most convenient for him to clean them: by this means, being less fit for stowage, they are not so saleable. The whole is then hurried away to the place where the agent is to receive his purchase; and when it comes there, the *Amildar* is astonished to find, that one half of what he had calculated upon is rejected, as being small, foul, or rent. The people are very docile; and the agent, so far as he has been able, has had the trees brought to him, just as they were cut, and freed from their branches and bark; and he has superintended the cutting them into billets of a convenient size, and the cleaning them properly from white wood. Owing to a want of time, he has been obliged to have them dried in the sun; and I observe, that in consequence of this a great many of the billets are rent in all directions. He suspects that the *Amildars* throw delays in his way, in order to force him to weigh the sandal while it is green. He thinks that, in order to instruct the villagers in the manner of cleaning the wood, it would be of advantage to send a carpenter, with proper tools, to each district.

"The agent says, that the sandal-wood of *Priya-pattana* and *Maha-Rayana-Durga*, although smaller, is of a much better quality than that of *Naggara*, which is inferior to that even of the districts south from *Priya-pattana*. None, or at least a very inconsiderable quantity, grows in *Coorg*, and *Bynadu*; but in *Tippoo's* reign the *Telicherry* market was chiefly supplied by the *Rajas* of these two countries, to whom it was smuggled by the inhabitants of *Mysore*, for the most violent orders had been issued prohibiting the sale. The people of *Coorg* understand the preparation of sandal-wood much better than those of *Mysore*. The proper manner, according to the agent, is as follows: the trees ought to be felled in the wane of the moon; the bark should be taken off immediately, and the trees cut into billets two feet long. These should be then buried in a piece of dry ground for two months, during which time the white ants will eat up all the outer wood, without touching the heart, which is the sandal. The billets ought then to be taken up and smoothed, and according to their size sorted into three kinds. The deeper the colour, the higher is the perfume; and hence the merchants sometimes divide sandal into red, yellow, and white; but these are all different shades of the same colour, and do not arise from any difference in the species of the tree. The nearer the root, in general, the higher is the perfume; and care should be taken, by removing the earth, to cut as low as possible. The billet nearest the root, when this has been done, is commonly called root-sandal, and is of a superior quality. In smoothing the billets, chips of the sandal are of course cut off, as are also fragments in squaring their ends. These chips and fragments, with the smallest assortment of billets, answer best for the Arabian market; and from them the essential oil is distilled. The largest billets are sent to China; and the middle-sized billets are used in India. The sandal, when thus prepared and sorted, for at least three or four months before it is sold, ought to be shut up from the sun and wind in close ware-houses; but the longer it is kept, with such precautions, the better; its weight diminishing more than its smell. Prepared in this way, it rarely either splits or warps, both of which accidents render it unfit for many of the purposes to which it is applied. If it be not buried in the ground, the entire trees ought to be brought into a shed at the warehouse, and there cut into proper billets, cleared of white wood, smoothed, and immediately shut up till thoroughly dry. The *Vir' Raja's* people, although they cure the sandal properly, have no notion of sorting it. The *Raja* is the principal dealer in this article, and insists on the merchants taking it good and bad, as it comes to hand, at the same price. He, no doubt, thus gets quit of the whole refuse; but, I believe, most merchants of experience would prefer selling their wares properly sorted.

"The officers of government say, that the sandal tree seldom or never grows in the lofty forests. It delights in the skirts of the open country, where small intervals are left between the fields, or on the banks of mountain torrents. It prefers a light stony soil, and such only as grows there is of any value. In the soil which this tree requires there is, however, something peculiar; as it rises up in one place copiously and not at all in another neighbouring spot, although there be no apparent difference in the situation or soil. It springs partly from seed, scattered by the birds that eat its berries; and partly from the roots of the trees, that have formerly been cut; and requires about twenty years to come to perfection. No pains, that I could discover, are taken to preserve the young plants from cattle; so that they always rise in a very straggling manner. If formerly any systematic management was observed, it has of late been entirely neglected. To prevent any person from cutting sandal without permission from government, laws have long existed: but these never were enforced with rigour by *Tippoo*. They are excessively severe, and prevent the peasantry from ever stealing the tree. It is only *Rajas*, and men above the law, that venture on this kind of theft. The present plan adopted by the *Dewan* seems to me to be the worst that could have been chosen. The woods are as much destroyed as if they had been sold to a renter; and, I am assured, will produce no more for at least twelve years; while no pains have been taken to make the most of what has been cut. To the conduct of this minister, however, no blame is, on this account, to be attached. He had sold the wood to the Company; and the misconduct of the officer, whom he had entrusted to cut it down, rendered it necessary for him to adopt the means by which he would be most likely enabled to fulfill his engagements, without attending to any other circumstance of less importance.

"Two means occur to me, as likely to ensure a considerable and regular income from sandal-wood. One means would be, to grant long leases to an individual, who would of course take every care of the trees, and employ every means proper to render what was cut fit for the market. The rent would be fixed at so much a year; and restrictive clauses, to prevent the renter from ruining the woods toward the end of his lease, would be necessary. The difficulty in exacting the performance of these restrictive clauses would make me prefer the other plan; which would be, to put the sandal-wood under the management of an agent, on a footing similar to the salt-agents of Bengal. He would preserve the trees, when young, by destroying all the other plants that might choke them, and by watching against thefts, or the encroachments of farmers. He would yearly cut the trees that were ripe, and no others. He would take care that the billets were properly prepared and cured; and he would bring the whole to public sale at proper times and places. His pay ought to be a commission on the neat proceeds. For some years, it is probable, the quantity procured would not overstock the market; but with care the quantity raised would, no doubt, so lower the price, as to diminish the profit very much. In that event, the sandal of the least profitable districts might be entirely destroyed; and in the most convenient and profitable situation, a sufficient quantity would be raised. As it is a mere article of luxury, or rather of ostentation, there can be no doubt of the propriety of making it entirely subservient to the purpose of raising a revenue; and the whole sandal of India is now in the hands of the Honourable Company, and the *Raja* of Mysore; between whom the necessary arrangements might be readily completed."

As Buchanan was travelling from HD Kote towards Nanjangud, and was passing through the neighbourhood of Hampapura (September 20, 1800), he had seen partially abandoned agricultural lands that were interspersed with sandal trees.

"20th September. – I went three cosses to *Humpa-pura*. The country has formerly been almost entirely cultivated; but at present about three fourths of it are waste. The sandal-wood is very common here, growing in intervals between the corn fields, and by the sides of torrents.---"

As regards the occurrence of sandal in the Kollegal region (in the East India Company's territory), which he had passed through on 3rd October, 1800, on way to Malabar (via Coimbatore), Buchanan provided the following information.

"**Sandalwood.** - In the *Coleagala* district are some sandal-wood trees, which are now cut by the collector, who employs a Mussulman agent. Fifteen years ago the *Sultan* cut the whole of the large trees. Like the sandal of *Magadi*, it thrives in the high forests of *Modhully* and *Maha-deveswara,* as well as in the skirts of the cultivated country; but it is not of so good a quality as that on the western frontier."

After completing his travel in the Malabar region, Buchanan entered Canara in the middle of the month of January, 1801. During his tour through Canara (during that period, Canara included the present districts of Dakshina Kannada, Udupi and Uttara Kannada, besides the Kasaragod district of Kerala State), Buchanan made very few references about sandalwood. Apparently, he was given to understand that sandal trees were not abundant in the forests or other localities in Canara. While camping at Mangalore (January 22-29, 1801), Buchanan had ascertained from the traders that although sandalwood was one of the commodities that were exported from Canara to Bombay it was all produce of the country above the *Ghats.* While camping at *Hulledy-pura* (Haldipur) (February 22-23, 1801), Buchanan had made enquiries with the principal traders about commercial activities in the Honnavar region. With regard to sandalwood he elicited the following information.

"*Hyder* sold to the Company the whole of the sandal wood. None of it is produced below the *Ghats*; and the quantity then brought annually to *Honawera* was from two to three hundred *Candies* of 600 lb."

Based on information furnished by Mr. Read, the collector of the northern division of Canara, Buchanan provided the following information regarding sandal trees and sandalwood in the division.

"**Sandal wood**. - 'All sandal trees,' says Mr. Read, 'growing upon private lands are considered as the property of the government; but it would be ridiculous to suppose, that they will always be considered as such by the occupiers of the estates, who undoubtedly commit frequent depredations upon them. It would therefore be for the benefit of the Company to have the whole cut down immediately that are of a fit age, which I am told is not till they are 30 years old. The whole might be easily collected at *Onore* (*Honawera*), and taken up by one of the Indiamen passing from *Bombay* to *China*.' Mr. Read was probably not aware, that last year all the ripe sandal in *Mysore* had been cut, and a great danger has consequently been incurred of glutting the market; while some years hence it will probably be greatly enhanced in value. I have already mentioned, that some measure should be adopted for regulating the cutting of the sandal wood; so that a certain supply should annually be brought to market, and no more permitted to grow than can be disposed of to advantage; for it must be considered as a mere superfluous luxury, the only proper use of which is to become a source of as much revenue as possible. As the Company and the *Mysore Raja* are in the sole possession of the countries which produce it, the arrangement might be readily made on somewhat like the following plan. An estimate of the quantity annually saleable, and of the whole produce that grows in both territories, having been formed, an agreement might be made, that each party should furnish the annual supply for a number of years, in proportion of the whole quantity that grows in his country. For instance, the *Mysore Raja* might furnish the supply for nineteen years, and the Company for one, which I imagine is somewhat about the relative proportion of what the two countries produce. The parties, of course, would be tied down to sell no more than a certain weight each year. They might improve its quality, as much as they could; and public sales, such as the Company use in *Bengal* for opium and salt, I am persuaded would be found by far the most advantageous manner of disposing of this article. Mr. Read mentions no difference in the quality of the sandal which grows below the *Ghats*, from that which grows in *Karnata*; but all the natives that I have ever spoken with on the subject, from *Pali-ghat* to this place, look upon the produce of the low country as of little or no value, as having no smell."

Although Canara did not appear to harbor much sandal trees below the *Ghats*, there were some above the *Ghats*. During his halt at Sirsi (March 15,

1801), Buchanan ascertained the following facts regarding sandal trees and sandalwood in the region.

> **"Sandal-wood**. - In the forests here, any person may cut whatever trees he pleases, except sandal-wood, and such as grow in forests producing pepper. The sandal trees are numbered, and put in charge of the head-man of the village. The custom of this district (*Taluc*) is, once in twelve years to cut the sandal. Three years ago a man purchased all that was fit for cutting, and procured about 100 *Maunds* of 40 *Seers* each, or about 21½ hundred-weight."

Towards the end of his journey through Canara, Mr. Read, the collector of the northern division of Canara, had furnished a detailed report to Buchanan regarding the production of various commodities in his division. In respect of goods procured from forest, Mr. Read had used the words 'The produce of the wastelands brought to market', as the concept of forest land as an administrative entity had not yet evolved. With regard to the annual production of sandalwood in terms of number of trees felled, Mr. Read provided the following information pertaining to the areas coming under his jurisdiction.

	Sandal wood trees. Total.
Kundapura	8758
Honawera	1017
Ancola	315
Supa	2097
Soonda, or Sudha	1718
Banawasi	3812
Billighy	5266

(**Note:** The administrative headquarters of Soonda or Sudha were at Sirsi)

Buchanan provided the following information regarding the presence of sandal trees in Shimoga district as he crossed over from Canara to the Mysore State (March 18, 1801).

"**Sandal wood**. - In this district (*Taluc*) there is some sandal-wood of a very good quality. It grows on dry hard ground, where of course the forest trees do not arrive at any great size. It is never planted, but grows from the seed which the birds disperse. In *Hyder's* government, in order to regulate the market properly, it was cut by officers of revenue (*Amildars*); and, after having been divided into proper billets, was sold on the account of government. *Purseram Bhow* cut all that he could, and the remainder was much injured by renting it out to merchants. All that was good for any thing was cut last year; but three years hence there will be some more fit for the market. The quantity procured last cutting was about 40 *Candies*, or 20 *Cutcha Maunds*, each weighing about 26 lb. Its price is commonly about 30 *Pagodas*, or 120 *Rupees*, a *Candy*. The following is considered to be the proper management. The trees, after having been cut, are allowed to remain in the woods for one month. They are then taken into a house; the white wood is removed, and the sandal, or heart, is cut into billets, and stored. The roots are dug up, and oil can be extracted from them, as well as from the chips, and the cuttings of the stem. All the persons who extract the oil are Mussulmans."

(**Note:** *Purseram Bhow* was a Maratha general who had invaded the country in the past.)

During his camp at *Sagar* (March 21, 1801) near *Ikkeri*, Buchanan ascertained from the merchants that the exports from Sagar were betel-nut, pepper and sandal-wood. He was also informed that 'the sandal wood of the *Ikeri Rayada* is superior to that of either the south or east.'

While camping at *Nagara* (March 25-27, 1801), Buchanan ascertained from the merchants that the chief exports of the region were pepper, betel-nut, sandal-wood, and cardamoms. Buchanan further mentioned that the *Marattha* merchants purchased sandal-wood from Nagara besides pepper and cardamoms. The merchants from Mangalore used to bring a number of products such as salt, rice, Horse-gram, coco-nuts, oil, turmeric, and sandal-wood from below the *Ghats* to Nagara. [This appears interesting, as the Canara region below the *Ghats* was not known for production of sandalwood.]

On April 1, 1801, as Buchanan was traveling from Mandagadde towards Shimoga, he came across a forest containing sandal trees.

> "East from the plain of *Manday Gudday*, I passed through a forest which contains much sandal-wood, but no *Teak*. Indeed, I have never seen the two trees in the same place."

Buchanan mentioned about the presence of sandal and jala (*Shorea talura*) trees in a hill called *Hiricul* situated near *Garuda-giri* (present Garudanagiri in Hassan district) which he had passed by on 9th May, 1801 while travelling from Hosadurga towards Banavara.

> "In a hill lying south from *Garuda-giri*, and called *Hiricul*, there are found both sandal-wood and lac. Owing to the increasing number of tigers, the collecting of this last has of late been given up."

On 15th May, 1801, while travelling from *Bailuru* (Belur) to *Hasina* (Hassan), Buchanan had noticed sandal trees growing on hedges around betel-nut gardens near a place called *Haltoray* (Halthore).

> "Sandal-wood trees are planted in the hedges that surround these gardens. The government has the sole right of cutting and disposing of this article of commerce; but the proprietor of the garden expects for his trouble in rearing it, and with justice receives, a gratuity. The planted *Sandal* is here reckoned of as good a quality as that which has grown spontaneously."

During his return journey to Madras, Buchanan passed by two sandal-bearing forests near Halagur (*Hulluguru*) on 9th June, 1801:

> "There are in this neighbourhood two hills producing sandal wood: *Basawana-Betta*, in the *Malawully* district, from which this year were procured 250 trees; and *Capala-durga*, which procured somewhat less. No more will be obtainable for eight years. On these hills there are no valuable timber trees, but abundance of *bamboos*."

The above descriptions recorded by Buchanan throw a good deal of light on the status of sandal trees and trade of sandalwood across large parts of Mysore state and Canara that were prevalent during the period just prior to the advent of the British. It may be noted that these descriptions are based on Buchanan's personal observations and on information that he had elicited from people with experience and knowledge about various aspects of sandal trees including the characteristics of growth of the species, processing and marketing of sandalwood, etc. He had critically analyzed different aspects with regard to the methods of extraction and processing of sandalwood, issues related to sustainable and regulated supply of sandalwood in order to attract reasonable price and to prevent glut in the market. He also commented upon the then prevailing ills of administration such as corruption and smuggling which resulted in loss of production and leakage of revenue, and in denying the rightful dues to the poor labourers engaged in felling of sandal trees, conversion and curing of sandalwood, etc. In a few instances, he had given positive suggestions with a view to improving efficiency in production and processing, and in augmenting profit from sandalwood trade.

Although Tipu Sultan is credited with declaring the sandal tree as a 'Royal tree', Buchanan's descriptions give an indication that sandal had enjoyed special status even prior to Tipu's reign. Buchanan's mention of having seen 20-year-old sandal trees on private land at Malur is indicative of the fact that even Tipu's father Hyder Ali had encouraged planting of sandal trees. [**Note**: Hyder Ali is credited with the construction of a fortified Sandal Koti at Srirangapatna; this building was intact for many years, being used by the British as a prison in the pre-Independence days, especially for keeping the freedom fighters in captivity. Subsequently, after the Independence in 1947, the building was converted and used as Government High School for some time.]

It is interesting to note from Buchanan's observation made during his tour between Belur and Hassan (May 15, 1801) that a system of payment of gratuity to the grower of sandal trees in private land was in vogue during those days in some form, although the details are not available. This system was formally reintroduced in the Mysore State much later, after more than hundred years, when the Sandal Bonus Rules were framed during the Conservatorship of *Rao Bahadur* M. Muthanna.

The general impression that emerges from Buchanan's descriptions is that the sandal tree grows best in dry, stony areas and that rich soil with good moisture content does not necessarily produce the best quality sandalwood with high oil content (perfume) though the tree may grow faster. It has also been mentioned that sandal does not grow in high forest but comes up well along the borders of such forests. At the same time, however, it has been mentioned a number of times that in the Mysore State sandalwood of the best quality came from the Nagara region (which primarily comprised present Shivamogga and Chikkamagaluru districts) and from the region around HD Kote near the borders of Coorg State. These areas situated in the Western *Ghats* region are generally favored with better soil and also relatively higher rainfall. It has also been mentioned that the sandal grown around Ikkeri (situated near Sagar in the present Shivamogga district) was better than that grown in the east and south. Thus the best quality sandal trees were obtained from areas receiving fairly high rainfall and generally harboring better soil. The above somewhat contradictory impressions regarding the growth of sandal continued during the subsequent years also and are prevalent even today.

It also emerges from Buchanan's descriptions that, although sandalwood was a state property and the King had full monopoly over it, there was some sort of parallel movement of sandalwood in the market. It is quite likely that although the lion's share of the sandalwood used to go to the *sandal kotis*, some quantity found way to the normal market. Apparently, the administrative system for harvest and collection of sandalwood was not foolproof and there were flexibility and weaknesses in the system resulting in leakages and pilferages, sometimes in connivance with the concerned officials; smuggling of sandalwood was also not uncommon.

Although the areas of Canara below the *Ghats* were not well-known for harboring sandal, Mr. Read's comments as quoted by Buchanan and also the tabular statement that Mr. Read had furnished giving details of extracted sandal trees indicate that some quantities of sandalwood were indeed produced in that region. The fact that some sandalwood was exported from below the *Ghats* of Canara to Nagara also indicates the same. It is quite likely that, as sandalwood from Nagara used to fetch better prices in the market, it was quite natural for the merchants from Nagara to buy material coming from other places at lower prices and resell it at higher prices along with the locally produced material.

It may be noted that when Buchanan had seen sandal trees for the first time at Malur after entering the Mysore State, he had found sandal trees and seegekai (*Acacia concinna*) climbers having been planted together around a castle. Seegekai is a very thorny climber, and hedges formed with such climbers are almost impenetrable. Thus the seegekai climbers provided protection not only to the castle but also to the sandal trees. Incidentally, sandal trees have one special characteristic: it is a semi-parasite and depends on other plants through haustorial connection for partial fulfillment of its nutritional requirement. This characteristic of sandal tree was discovered much later - towards the end of the nineteenth century. Many leguminous plants including *Acacias* are known as good host plants for sandal. However, whether the decision to plant sandal and seegekai together at Malur almost a century earlier was a mere coincidence or because of some ancient wisdom is anybody's guess.

Chapter 3

TEAK IN MYSORE AND CANARA

During his travel in Mysore and Canara, Buchanan came across teak trees for the first time in the forests of *Savana-durga* in Magadi which he had visited during the period June 15-19, 1800. While giving the details of various trees found in these forests, Buchanan wrote about teak as follows:

> *"Doda Tayca, Tectona robusta.* A few trees of this valuable timber are found in most places of this hilly tract; but in general they do not grow to be of a size sufficient for use. Some good timber may, it is said, be procured at *Mutati Habigay*, a place near *Capala-durga.*"

> [**Note:** The accepted/preferred scientific name of teak is *Tectona grandis*, Linnaeus. Buchanan in his book had used the name *Tectona robusta*.]

Buchanan mentioned about the presence of plenty of teak trees in the forests of Heggadadevankote which he had visited during September 16-18, 1800. While giving the details of various trees found in these forests located in the foothills of the Western *Ghats*, Buchanan wrote about the presence of teak as follows:

> *"1. Doda Tayca. Tectona robusta.* In great plenty."

Buchanan mentioned about the presence of teak in the forests of Kollegal through which he had passed on October 3, 1800, on his way to Malabar via Coimbatore.

> "**Forests**. - The greater part of the mountains in this district produce only stunted trees, or bushes. *Mod-hully* and *Maha-deveswara* are the only ones that are clothed with timber trees; but in size these are greatly inferior to those of the western *Ghats*. Some teak and *Biriday* of a good size may be procured."

[*Biriday* was the local name of *Dalbergia latifolia*.]

On 7th October, 1800, after reaching Hanur from Singanallur, Buchanan wrote about a hill called *Hediny Betta* as follows:

> "The principal hill between the *Cavery* and the southern extremity of the eastern *Ghats* is called *Hediny Betta*; and on this chiefly grow the timber trees that are to be procured. It produces chiefly *Tayka*, *Biriday*, *Whonay*, and *Jala*, which have all been before mentioned. The sandal wood grows on a hill called *Mahadeveswara*."

Buchanan had also mentioned about the occurrence of teak in the forests of the southern part of Canara. As he was traveling beyond Bantwal on February 1, 1801, he had come across teak trees in the forests on the high hills and described in the following words.

> "*1st February*. – I went three cosses to *Cavila-cutty*. The hills are much higher than those to the westward, and some of them are covered with tall thick forests, in which are found *Teak* (*Theka*) and wild *Mango* (*Mangifera*) trees, and the palm which Linnaeus called *Caryota*. -----."

While travelling in the eastern part of *Mirzee* (Mirjan) in northern Canara on 25th February, 1801, Buchanan had mentioned thus: 'So far as I went, no *Teak* grows in these forests; but I am told, that it is procurable further inland'. Apparently, teak was rare in the coastal zone but occurred in the interior forests to the east. Buchanan did not come across teak trees near Gopshitta (*Gopi-chitty*) which he had passed through on 4th March, 1801: 'In many places here, the soil seems good, and the trees are tall; so that pepper might probably be cultivated to advantage. In many other places the hills are barren, producing nothing but bushes, or stunted trees: among them I saw no *Teak*.' Buchanan mentioned about the spontaneous occurrence of teak and other trees in the forest near *Barabuli* (March 8, 1801): 'two species of *Artocarpus, Teak*, blackwood, *Cassia*, wild-nutmegs, *Caryota urens*, and the *Bassia*, with perhaps some others that escaped my notice.' While travelling near *Cutaki* (Kattige) on 9th March, 1801, Buchanan had mentioned that teak became common about midway up the *Ghats*, but the trees were very inferior in size as compared with the other hardwood species of the terrain. He had also mentioned about the abundant availability of 'the *Teak* in some parts of this district *Yella-pura*' which, 'in the rainy season may be floated down the river.' After ascertaining from the Tahsildar of *Yella-pura*, Buchanan mentioned (March 10, 1801) that "In the eastern parts towards *Hully-halla, Sambrany, Mandanuru, Mundagodu*, and *Induru*, the woods consist mostly of *Teak*, and there are no gardens." During his travel from *Sersi* to *Banawasi* on 16th March, 1801, Buchanan had noticed some teak in a stately forest in which the pepper-vine grew spontaneously.

Reference about the presence of teak in the forests on the bank of the Tunga River was made by Buchanan as he was travelling from Tudur towards Shimoga on 1st April, 1801.

> "*1st April*. - I went four cosses to *Baikshavani Mata*. The road is near the left bank of the *Tunga*. After leaving the cultivated country near *Tuduru*, which is pretty extensive, I entered a forest of trees and *Bamboos*, almost equalling in stature those of the western *Ghats*. Here were many fine *Teak* trees, more indeed than I have ever seen in any one place. They might be of value, could they be floated down the *Tunga* to the *Krishna*, and so to the sea; which I think might probably be done by supporting the floats with *Bamboos*. The *Tunga* at all times contains water; but in the dry season the channel, being full of rocks, will not admit floats. In the

rainy season the river swells prodigiously, and is said to be in most places eight or ten feet higher than the top of the rocks. Its stream is then exceedingly rapid and muddy, and filled with large trees swept away by the flood; while in some places rocks come very near the surface. These circumstances would, no doubt, render the navigation in boats very dangerous, but they do not seem to me likely to impede well-constructed floats of timber, strengthened and buoyed up by *Bamboos*. If this should be found practicable, I know of no place that would answer better, for rearing a *Teak* forest, than the banks of the *Tunga* near *Tuduru*, where close to the river there is much excellent soil, which is considered as useless. As there are already on the spot many fine *Teak* trees, all that would be required would be, to eradicate the trees of less value, which I look upon as a necessary step to procure any considerable quantity of *Teak* in a well regulated government. In the wilds of *America*, or the dominions of *Ava*, where a few inhabitants are buried in the recesses of an immense forest, a considerable supply of timber may without trouble be procured; but in a well cultivated country, without much pains bestowed on rearing the proper trees, it is in vain to think of supplying the extensive demands of the ship-builder."

Buchanan also mentioned about the presence of teak trees nearer to Shimoga town: "*2ⁿᵈ April.* - I went a long stage, called five cosses, to *Shiva-mogay*. The first two cosses of this road are in a forest of very fine trees, many of which are *Teak.*-----"

Buchanan's diaries reveal that he had come across fairly well-grown teak trees in the forests of Shimoga and HD Kote. He also came across some teak trees of stunted or moderate growth in the Savanadurga and Kollegal forests. As regards Canara, although he had seen some fine and some stunted teak trees, they were not wide-spread; however, he had been told about the presence of good teak trees in the forests of Yellapur, Haliyal, Mundgod, etc. The best teak forests of Canara occurred in the climax moist deciduous forests, mostly located in parts of Supa, Haliyal, Kirwatti, Mundgod, etc. through which Buchanan had not travelled. His travel route was mainly through evergreen, semi-evergreen and patches of secondary moist deciduous forests which normally do not harbor natural teak. The fact that Canara had abundant teak trees becomes evident from the following tabular information regarding annual extraction of teak and rosewood trees that Buchanan had received from Mr. Read, the collector of the northern division of Canara.

	Teak trees cut annually.	*Sissa* **trees cut annually.**
Kundapura	-	1582
Honawera	2059	344
Ancola	1124	572
Supa	394495	59770
Soonda, or Sudha	1639	1715
Banawasi	29	3069
Billighy	-	34

The above table indicates that within a decade of acquiring Canara, the British had started large-scale extraction of teak and rosewood trees from the forests of Supa, which now correspond to the teak forests of Gund, Virnoli, Dandeli, Kulgi, Joida, etc. Presence of teak in the other parts of Canara was relatively less, but some quantities of rosewood were present throughout.

Chapter 4

BAMBOO IN MYSORE AND CANARA

Dr. Buchanan left Madras for Srirangapatna on the afternoon of April 23, 1800. He was to travel via Vellore and Bangalore. On the second day of his journey i.e. on April 24, he arrived at the *Saymbrumbacam* tank, a very large water body which irrigated paddy fields of thirty-two adjacent villages. Buchanan narrated the very good works done by the late Collector, Mr. Place, during whose administration the tank had been repaired, in the following words.

"The late collector, Mr. Place, although he augmented the revenue considerably, by the repairs made on this tank during his administration, gave great satisfaction to the inhabitants. Another of Mr. Place's measures seems to have been very well judged. He caused each village to be surrounded by a hedge of *Bamboos*, with two small towers at each gate. By this measure, in case of any invasion, small parties of plundering cavalry may be kept off, and a great quantity of that most valuable plant *bamboo* will in time be raised. At present it is brought from the neighbourhood of *Tripetty*, and sells three-fold dearer than at *Calcutta*: for from ten to sixteen *Bamboos* cost here a *Pagoda*, or 7*s.* 4¼*d.*"

In the Mysore State, Buchanan came across bamboo for the first time in the forests near Channapatna which he described as follows:

> "**14**[th] ***May. Forests***. – I went to *Chinapatam*, or *Chinapatana*, through a very beautiful country, consisting of swelling grounds, in some places cultivated, and in many more covered with trees, which are intermixed with steep fantastic rocks and hills. The trees here are by far the finest that I have seen in either *Carnatic*, although they fall very short of the stately forests of *Chittagong*. In these woods the *bamboo* is common. It is now in flower, and produces a great quantity of grain, which is gathered for food by the poor inhabitants of the neighbourhood."

While traveling through Magadi on 13th June, 1800, Buchanan saw some good forests harboring bamboos.

> "------. The higher parts are covered with trees, which, owing to the poverty of the soil, are in most places very small; but near *Savana-durga*, and in a few other parts, the timber and *Bamboos* grow to a good size.-----."

On the same day (June 13, 1800), when Buchanan had visited an iron forge, he had noticed that charcoal prepared from bamboo was used in the furnace for the purpose of heating. Apparently, charcoal prepared from bamboo was the most preferred for iron smelting (Vol. II; Chapter 7; Page No. 17).

On 15th June, 1800, Buchanan had noticed spontaneous growth of bamboo and other trees in a place in a more or less abandoned state; this place had formerly contained several temples and some large gardens belonging to *Magadi Kempe Gowda*. He described as follows:

> "A few families of *Brahmans* remain near the ruinous temples; and the site of the gardens is evident from a number of fruit and flowering trees. Every other part of the enclosure is overgrown with forest trees and *Bamboos.*"

After visiting the forests of *Savana-durga* in Magadi (June 15-19, 1800), Buchanan gave a detailed account of the various tree species found in the forests and their important uses. With regard to bamboo, he gave the following account.

> **"Bideru, Bambusa**. The *Bamboo* here is divided into two kinds: one solid, or nearly so, and is called by the natives *Chittu*; the other hollow, and called *Doda*. They are not considered as distinct species, the solidity of the former being attributed to its slow growth in dry stony places. Not having had an opportunity of examining the fructification, I cannot determine how far this opinion is well founded. It is the only kind found among these hills; and, although not of great size, is very strong and heavy. For common purposes I do not think it is so useful as the hollow kind; but it is admirably adapted for the shafts of spears, and by *Tippoo* was applied to that use for his cavalry."

From the above description of Buchanan, it appears that during that time the local people had presumed two species of bamboos to be one and the same. From the description of the species, it is apparent that the two species were *Bambusa bambos/arundinacea* (Dowga/hollow bamboo) and *Dendrocalamus strictus* (Medri/solid bamboo).

Buchanan had also mentioned about the occurrence of bamboo in the Nandi-durga hills (July 17, 1800).

> "Among the hills of *Nandi-durga* is much fertile land, now covered with *Bamboos*, and useless trees; but which, with a little encouragement, might be brought into cultivation: this, however, would be improper, until there be a number of people, and a quantity of stock, sufficient to occupy all lands that have formerly been cultivated, but are now waste. Such, at least, is the opinion of the *Amildar*, who is a sensible man."

While providing details of trees found in the forests in the foothills of the Western *Ghats* near *Hegodu Devana Cotay* (presently HD Kote) which he visited during September 16-18, 1800, Buchanan mentioned about bamboo as follows:

"*Bamboos.* Large, but not solid."

The above remark indicates that the bamboo growing in the HD Kote region was dowga bamboo (*Bambusa bambos*).

On 7th October, 1800, while travelling through the Company's territory of Kollegal, Buchanan mentioned that the forest-dwelling tribesmen called *Soliga* collected various items such as timber, bamboo, honey, yam, etc. from the forest and supplied these to the farmers.

On 5th March, 1801, while traveling in Canara, Buchanan had come across a forest near *Caderi* (Kadra) where bamboo was the most common plant among others.

"The most common is the prickly *Bamboo*, called *Colaki.*"

Buchanan was highly impressed with the forests of the Western *Ghats* that he passed through as he traveled on 9th March, 1801, near *Cutaki* (Kattige) on way to Yellapur. He described the excellent growth of the trees and bamboos in the following words.

Soil and trees of the western Ghats

"Here the western *Ghats* assume an appearance very different from that at *Pedda Nayakana Durga*, or *Kaveri-pura*. The hills, although steep and stony, are by no means rugged, or broken with rocks: on the contrary, the stones are buried in a rich mould, and in many places are not to be seen without digging. Instead, therefore, of the naked, sun-burnt, rocky peaks, so common in the eastern *Ghats*, we here have fine mountains clothed with the most stately forests. I have no where seen finer trees, nor any *Bamboos* that could be compared with those which I this day observed. The *Bamboos* compose a large part of the forest, grow in detached clumps, with open spaces between, and equal in height the *Caryota urens*, one of the most stately palms, of which also there is great plenty. ------."

During his return journey to Madras, Buchanan on 9th June, 1801, passed by two sandal-bearing forests with abundance of bamboos near Halagur (*Hulluguru*).

"There are in this neighbourhood two hills producing sandal wood: *Basawana-Betta*, in the *Malawully* district, from which this year were procured 250 trees; and *Capala-durga*; which procured somewhat less. No more will be obtainable for eight years. On the hills there are no valuable timber trees, but abundance of *bamboos*."

Although Buchanan had on a number of occasions come across bamboo in the forests of various parts of Mysore and Canara, he did not mention about how bamboo was utilized by the people. Apparently, the solid bamboo (medri bamboo) did not have much use other than as spear-handle used by the cavalry. He also did not mention about whether people were planting bamboos in their farmlands. Bamboo did not appear to have received sufficient attention of the farmer as a species that could be planted in a corner of his homestead or along the border of his farmland.

Chapter 5

OTHER ECONOMICALLY
IMPORTANT TREES

On four occasions during the course of his journey in Mysore and Canara, Buchanan had given fairly detailed information about the trees occurring in the forests that he had passed through. Buchanan would usually scrutinize the tree specimens that were brought to him. He would also enquire about the various uses of the trees from the local people. Whenever there was difference between his perceptions or knowledge about the tree and what was told to him by the local people, he would incorporate his reservation while commenting on the tree species. The four forest areas that Buchanan had visited along with the dates of visit were as follows: (1) Savanadurga forests in Magadi (June 15-19, 1800); (2) forests in the foothills of the Western *Ghats* near Heggadadevankote (September 16-18, 1800); (3) forests near *Caderi* (Kadra) in Canara below the *Ghats* on March 5, 1801; and (4) forests near *Cutaki* (Kutteggy/Kattige) in Canara above the *Ghats* (March 9, 1801). The trees as described by Buchanan and his comments on each tree species, along with their present scientific and local names, in respect of the four forest areas mentioned above have been tabulated and are placed at **Annexure Nos. I, II, III and IV**, respectively. Perusal of these tabular statements would reveal that majority of the trees were useful to the people in one way or another. While most of these trees provided timber for construction, furniture and agricultural or other implements, some had provided benefits such as gum, oil, fruits, flowers, cordage, tannins, medicines, etc. There were very few trees that did not have any utility. It is interesting to note that most of the trees which people had identified more than 200 years ago as trees yielding good or useful timber continue to be popular timber trees even today. People were also aware of certain specific tree species that would yield wood of a desirable trait. Important timber yielding tree species mentioned by Buchanan include the following: teak (*Tectona grandis*), beete/sissum (*Dalbergia latifolia*), honne (*Pterocarpus marsupium*), nandi (*Lagerstroemia lanceolata*), matti (*Terminalia tomentosa*), kindal/hunal (*Terminalia paniculata*), holematti/torematti (*Terminalia arjuna*), heddi (*Adina cordifolia*), kalam (*Mitragyna parviflora*), hadaga (*Cordia macleodii*), mashwal (*Chloroxylon swietenia*), kadamba (*Anthocephalus chinensis*), naviladi/bharanige (*Vitex altissima*), culi/shivani (*Gmelina arborea*), jalari (*Shorea talura*), neral (*Syzigium cumini*), bevu (*Azadirachta indica*), tupra (*Diospyros melanoxylon*), dindal/dindiga (*Anogeissus latifolia*), jamba (*Xylia xylocarpa*), sagadi (*Schleichera oleosa*), bilwara (*Albizia odoratissima*), bilijali (*Acacia leucophloea*), kaggali (*Acacia catechu*), mugali (*Acacia suma*), padri (*Stereospermum chelonoides*), hale/beppale (*Wrightia tinctoria*), kadunimbe (*Atalantia monophylla*), sampige (*Michelia champaca*), etc. Similar to teak, beete/sissum (*Dalbergia latifolia*) was also an important timber tree of that period. It appears to have had fairly wide-spread occurrence in the forests. Apparently, the town Bidadi (*Biridy* or *Wiridy*) situated near Bangalore derived its name from the Kannada name of the tree. (May 13, 1800; Vol. I.; Page No. 49)

Firewood and charcoal were two other important products from trees. Buchanan did not mention much about the use of firewood perhaps because it was the principal or rather the only source of domestic energy during the period of his visit to Mysore and Canara. He had, however, noticed the acute shortage of firewood at Srirangapatna and mentioned as follows:

> "Firewood at *Seringapatam* is a dear article, and the fewel most commonly used is cow-dung made up into cakes."

Firewood was also required extensively in most of the industrial activities including agro-processing works that involved heating or boiling. As regards charcoal, it was an important source of energy for industrial activities such as smelting of iron, manufacture of steel, glass making, etc.

that required heating material in an enclosed chamber (furnace) to very high temperatures. This will be discussed in some detail in *Chapter 8.*

In addition to the above tree-based products, a number of commodities that were traded or consumed locally were sourced from trees. These included *Lac* (*Shorea talura* - Jalari), *Terra Japonica* (*Acacia catechu* - Katha), Jaggery and Spirituous liquor (*Phoenix sylvestris – Ichalu*), *Seegekai* (*Acacia concinna*), etc. Besides, varieties of oil, gum, cordage, fruit, flower, flavoring agent, dye, medicine, etc. were obtained from trees/plants. Buchanan in his diaries had provided information about such trees and plants, some of his descriptions being quite elaborate. These are discussed in the following paragraphs.

Shorea talura (jala/jalari)

During his travel from Srirangapatna to Bangalore (second visit), Buchanan had spent a day (June 12, 1800) in and around *Rama-giri* (Ramanagara). Here Buchanan came to know that the *Shorea talura* (jala) tree was used as a host for breeding *Lac* insects to produce *Lac.* He described as follows:

> "**Lac.** - *Lac* is produced in several of the neighbouring hills, upon the tree called *Jala*, which seems to be of the same genus with the *Shorea* of Gaertner, and this is probably not different from the *Vatica* of Linnaeus. The tree is never planted, but grows naturally; and the persons who rent the *Lac* carry the insect from one tree to another. The tree grows to a large size; and there are a great many, on which no insects have been put. The *Chensu* and *Woddar* are the persons who commonly rent it; but they allege, they are discouraged from the employment, by the want of leases for a number of years. *Stick-lac* sells here at three *Fanams* for the *Maund* of 40 *Seers*, or 9*s.* 4½*d.* a hundred weight."

Buchanan came across the *Shorea talura* trees once again a few days later (June 15-19, 1800) as he passed through the forests of *Savana-durga* in Magadi. Here he mentioned the importance of the tree for its timber as well as for Lac production. He also commented on the dwindling production of Lac as a result of the local administration's insistence on short-term leases.

Buchanan had suggested for long-term leases to encourage people to take up Lac cultivation in order to boost production of the valuable article.

"Jala, Shorea Jala, Buch. MSS.

"Lac insects. - Here it grows only to a small size; but at *Rama-giri*, and many other places, it becomes large. It is said to take a polish, to be durable, and to be used for furniture. In *Mysore* it is on this tree only that the *Lac* insects breed. Formerly there were many trees near *Rama-giri* that contained *Lac*, and paid a considerable rent; but during the war carried on by Lord Cornwallis they were destroyed by the armies. Although there are now great numbers of the trees, none of the insects are reared. This is attributed to the want of leases. The *Amildar* was wont to let the trees for no longer than one year; it can therefore be no object for an individual to supply the trees with insects, as he would not be certain of enjoying the fruits of his labour. Some settled bargain for a number of years ought to be entered into with those who are willing to introduce such a valuable article of cultivation."

While passing through the hills of Nandi-durga (July 17, 1800) near Chikkaballapura in company with the local *Amildar*, Buchanan collected further information about the jala trees and Lac cultivation, and described in the following words.

"I took an opportunity, in company with this *Amildar*, of examining into the management of the *Lac* insect; and for this purpose we collected all the people who follow that employment. I have always found, that the more of any class of people were assembled, the more likely I was to get just information: not that all of them spoke; some one or two men generally answered my questions; but they did it without fear of reflexions from those who might otherwise have been absent; as everyone, if he chose, had an opportunity of speaking. The *Hindus* of all descriptions, so far as I have observed, are indeed very desirous of having every kind of business discussed in public assemblies.

"**Lac insect**. - The people who manage the *Lac* insect, near the hills of *Nandi-durga*, are of the cast *Woddaru*; and for the exclusive use of the trees they pay a rent to government. The tree on which the insect feeds is the *Jala*, which is nearly related to the *Saul* of Bengal, or the *Shorea* of Gaertner, and perhaps the *Vatica chinensis* of Linnaeus. All the trees that I saw here were small, not exceeding eight or ten feet in height; and their growth was kept down by the insect and its managers; for this size answers best. The tree, left to itself, grows to a large size, and is good timber. For feeding the insect, it thrives very well in a dry barren soil; and is not planted, but allowed to spring up spontaneously as nature directs. It is often chocked by other trees, and destroyed by *Bamboos*, which, by rubbing one against another, in this arid region, frequently take fire, and lay waste the neighbouring woods. By removing all other trees from the places where the *Jala* naturally grows, and perhaps by planting a few trees on some other hills, and protecting them from being chocked as they gradually propagate themselves, the *Lac* insect might be raised to any extent on lands now totally useless, and never capable of being rendered arable. In *Kartika*, or from about the middle of October to the middle of November, the *Lac* is ripe. At that time it surrounds almost every small branch of the tree, and destroys almost every leaf. The branches intended for sale are then cut off, spread out on mats, and dried in the shade. A tree or two, that are fullest of the insect, are preserved to propagate the breed; and of those a small branch is tied to every tree in the month of *Chaitra*, or from about the middle of March to the middle of April; at which time the trees again shoot out young branches and leaves. The *Lac* dried on the sticks is sold to the merchants of *Balahari, Gutti, Bangalore*, &c; and according to the quantity raised, and to the demand, varies in price, from 5 to 20 *Fanams* a *Maund*. This is what is called *stick-lac*. In my account of *Bangalore*, I have given the process of dyeing with this substance; which, after the dye has been extracted, is formed into *seed* and *shell lac*."

The hills in the vicinity of Madhugiri had harbored large numbers of *Shorea talura* trees. During his halt in Madhugiri (July 25-29, 1800),

Buchanan had ascertained the following information about the production of lac in the region.

> "**Lac.** – From the hills in this vicinity, about a hundred *Maunds* of *lac* (almost 24 hundred weight) are annually procured; and there is more in several of the neighbouring districts."

Buchanan mentioned about the presence of *Jala* trees in the foothills of the Western *Ghats* near *Hegodu Devana Cotay* (presently HD Kote) which he visited during September 16-18, 1800. He also mentioned that these were large timber-yielding trees and were not used for Lac cultivation there: "32. *Jala. Shorea Jala* Buch. MSS. A large timber tree. No *lac* is made here."

Buchanan mentioned about the presence of jala and sandalwood trees in a hill called *Hiricul* situated south of *Garuda-giri* (present Garudanagiri in Hassan district) which he had passed by on May 9, 1801 while travelling from Hosadurga towards Banavara. He had been informed that collection of lac from the jala trees had been discontinued since the previous year owing to the increasing number of tigers.

Acacia catechu (kutch/katha)

In his travel diaries, Buchanan had mentioned a number of times about *Terra japonica* or *Katha* which was an important article of trade during those days. It was derived from the heartwood of the *Acacia catechu* (kaggali/kutch) tree. During his travel within the Mysore State, Buchanan had nowhere mentioned about having seen katha being manufactured. Although he had mentioned about the presence of the kaggali tree in the forests of Savanadurga and Channapatna in Mysore State, he had categorically indicated that it was not the tree from which *Catechu* was produced.

> "*Cagali, Mimosa catechu*, Roxb. Pl. Cor. N. 174. In some places, as near *Chinapatam*, this grows to be a large crooked tree. The quality of the timber is good. It is not the tree which produces the *Catechu*."

He had also found the tree in the forests in the foothills of the Western *Ghats* near *Hegodu Devana Cotay* (presently HD Kote) (September 16-18, 1800) but did not mention anything regarding the extraction of *Catechu.*

"7. *Cagali. Mimosa Catechu* Roxb. Fl. Cor. N. 174. Grows in the skirts of the forest only, and never reaches to a large size."

However, during his travel through Canara, Buchanan had obtained firsthand information about the manufacture of katha in a place called Chandya, near Ankola (March 1, 1801). He provided the following information.

"**Catechu.** – In this part of *Kankana*, a little *Cut, Catechu,* or *Terra Japonica*, is made by some poor people, who gave me the following account of the process. The tree, or *Mimosa Catechu*, is called here *Keiri*, and grows spontaneously on all the hills of *Kankana*, but no where else in the peninsula that I observed. It is felled at any season; and, the white wood being removed, the heart is cut into small bits, and put, with one half the quantity of water by measure, into a round-bellied earthen pot. It is then boiled for about three hours; and when the decoction has become ropy, it is decanted. The same quantity of water is again added, and boiled, until it becomes ropy; when it is decanted, and a third water also is given. This extracts all the substance from the wood. The three decoctions are then mixed, and next morning boiled in small pots, until the extract becomes thick, like tar. It is afterwards allowed to remain in the pots for two days, and then has become so hard, that it will not run. Some husks of rice are then spread on the ground, and the inspissated juice is formed into balls, about the size of oranges, which are placed on the husks, or on leaves, and dried seven days in the sun. For two months afterwards they are spread out in the shade to dry, or in the rainy season for twice that length of time, and are then fit for sale. Merchants who live above the *Ghats* advance the whole price four months before the time of delivery, and give 2 *Rupees* for a *Maund* of 40 *Cutcha Seers* of 24 *Rupees* weight; that is, for a hundred-weight 9 89/100 Rupees, or nearly 1*l.* sterling. The merchants who purchase reside chiefly in *Darawara, Shanore,* and other parts in that neighbourhood, and are those who supply the greater part of the peninsula with the article, which among the natives is in universal use. Their greatest supply comes from that part of *Kankana* which is subject to the *Marattahs.* The encouragement of this manufacture in British *Kankana* seems to merit attention. The tree is exactly the same with what I found used for the like purpose in the dominions of *Ava,* and does not agree very well with the descriptions in the *Supplementum Plantarum* of the younger Linnaeus, nor in Dr. Roxburgh's manuscripts."

Acacia concinna (seegekai)

On his maiden journey from Madras to Srirangapatna (via Bangalore), while passing through Malur on 7th May, 1800, Buchanan had visited a castle the outer wall of which had a strong hedge of seegekai (*Acacia concinna*) climbers along with sandal trees. Buchanan had indicated that *Shicai,* the fruit of *Mimosa saponaria* (former name of *Acacia concinna*) was used as soap for washing the hair. He also mentioned that the acidic leaves of the plant were used by the poor as a substitute for tamarind which was a common souring agent used in the cookery of the southern Hindus. 'The hedge is rented at 20 *Pagodas* (*6l. 4s.7d.*) a year; for the fruit is an article of trade, that is carried even so far as Madras, where three pods are said to cost 1 *dub,* or small *pice.*'

During his evening walk in the woods near Bidadi (then known as *Wiridy* or *Biridy*) on 13th May, 1800, Buchanan was shown a number of trees as being useful. These included the species *Mimosa pennata* whose present name is *Acacia pennata,* its local name being kaadu seegekai. Buchanan described the species as follows:

> "*Ha-Shi-Cai, Mimosa pennata.* It is a favourite food of the long-legged goat of this country."

Phoenix sylvestris (ichala/wild date)

During his travel, Buchanan came across *Phoenix sylvestris* (ichala) trees a number of times in the relatively dry tracts of the Mysore State. The scientific name of the tree during Buchanan's time was *Elate sylvestris*. Buchanan described the tree in some detail in view of its wide-spread presence as well as its importance as a revenue earner for the State. The tree was well-known for its juice which was extracted for making spirituous liquor known as *Toddy/Tari* and also a special kind of jaggery.

While travelling from Bangalore to Srirangapatna, Buchanan came across *Phoenix sylvestris* (ichala) trees near *Muduru* (Maddur) on 15th May, 1800.

> "**Wild date**. - Among the waste lands there are many parts that seem capable of being rendered arable. In several places the *Phoenix farinifera*, Roxb: abounds; and intermixed with it, the *Elate sylvestris,* or wild date. From this the inhabitants extract *Tari*, or *Toddy*, in the same manner as is practised in *Bengal.* Here the *Tari* is used for drinking only; but in some places, where it is more plenty, it is boiled down into a hard substance called *Jogory*, which by the poor is substituted in place of the Jagory extracted from the sugar-cane."

On the next day (May 16, 1800), as he was travelling towards Mandya, Buchanan passed through a terrain that mostly comprised wasteland covered with brushwood interspersed with *Phoenix farinifera* and *Elate sylvestris.*

> "16th *May.* **Appearance of the country**. - I went to *Mundium*, through a country free from hills, but of which not more than one half is arable. Much of it, however, might be rendered so, without difficulty. The soil is in general poor. The waste land is occupied by brushwood, and many places are covered with the *Phoenix farinifera*, Roxb. among which are some trees of the wild date.

"Wild date. - It is reported, that this tree was formerly very common; but *Tippoo*, observing that his subjects frequently intoxicated themselves with the *Tari*, ordered the whole to be cut down; and in places near the capital the order was enforced."

During his travel in the neighbourhood of Madhugiri (July 25, 1800), Buchanan had come across many trees of wild date (*Elate sylvestris*). Here, he gave a fairly detailed description about various aspects of the tree such as its natural regeneration and growth, the manner in which the trees were rented out, and the method of extraction of its juice and preparation of *Toddy*, etc.

"Wild date, or *Elate sylvestris* - From the seed dropped by birds, or by accident, great numbers of the palm called *Ejalu* (*Elate sylvestris*) grow here wild. It will thrive on any good soil that does not contain lime, and grows indeed on the poorest lands; but in these it affords hardly any juice. To rear it requires no trouble, as the prickly nature of its leaves sufficiently deters cattle. The English use only one name for the juices of all the different palm-trees in India, and call them all *Toddy*, which seems to be a corruption of *Tari*, the Mussulman name for the juice of the *Palmira*, or *Borassus flabelliformis*. The natives have distinct names for each kind of juice; and, in fact, there seem to be considerable differences in their qualities. That of the *Elate* is by the Mussulmans called *Sindy*, in the *Karnata* language *Henda*; and in the *Telinga* and *Tamul* dialects *Callu*. The juice of the *Borassus*, although the tree grows well enough, is here never extracted, and the natives deny their extracting *Sindy*. The *Sindy* is never drunk by the natives till it has fermented, when it becomes exceedingly intoxicating, and in many villages great quantities are consumed. In this place it is never distilled; though, no doubt, it would afford a spirit that, by rectification and age, might be made palatable. Much of the *Sindy*, when fresh, is boiled down into *Jagory*, which sells for about 1/3 of the price of that made from sugar-cane, and is chiefly used for distillation. The process here is exactly the same as that described at *Waluru*. [**Note:** The process of distillation appears in *Chapter 8* of this book.]

"Manner of letting these palms – All the *Ejalu* palms in this district are let to a person of the *Idiga* cast, who pays annually 120 *Pagodas*, or rather more than 40*l.* and lets them out again to the *Idigas* of the different villages. Each palm gives juice for three months in the year, and they will do this at any season; so that every man divides his trees into four portions, and thus has throughout the year a regular supply and employment.

"The juice of the *Elate sylvestris* is extracted by cutting a deep horizontal gash into the stem, at some distance below the leaves, and then cutting towards this from below in a sloping direction. The juice exudes from the pores of the sloping surface, and is collected in a notch formed at its lower extremity; whence it is conveyed into a pot by one of the divisions of the leaf, which serves as a gutter. According to his alertness, one man can collect the juice of from 30 to 50 palms. 50 good trees, or 100 bad ones, give 70 *Pucka Seers*, or about 17 ale gallons; and this may be boiled into 70 *Cucha Seers* of *Jagory*, or about 46½ *lb.* At sun-rise it is put in earthen pots, and boiled until noon. When the ebullition becomes so violent as to endanger the running over of the liquor, it is allayed by a small quantity of *Ricinus* seed. Small holes are then made in the ground, and in the bottom of each are placed two cuttings of any twining plant. Over these are laid some leaves, upon which the boiling *Jagory* is poured. When it has cooled, it is lifted out by means of the projecting ends of the twining plant. This palm is of very little other use. Mats are made of its leaves, and its stem is used in building the wretched huts of the poorer class of inhabitants."

As Buchanan proceeded towards Sira (July 30, 1800), he passed through abandoned agricultural lands interspersed with barren hills. In these areas also, he came across wild date palm trees. While describing the appearance of the country, he wrote about these trees as follows:

"----. A great part of the country is covered with wild date palm, or *Elate sylvestris*, of which no care is taken. Even on bad soils it seems to be so thriving, that I have no doubt but that even there it is sufficiently productive of juice."

While travelling from Nagamangala towards Melkote (August 28, 1800), Buchanan came across very barren land interspersed with low rocky hills, some parts of which were covered with low trees, especially with the *Elate sylvestris*, or wild date.

During his trip from Srirangapatna to Periyapatna, Buchanan passed through barren lands (September 8, 1800) that in the past had been cultivated but abandoned subsequently due to invasions followed by famine. In these areas also Buchanan saw 'a few spots covered with the *Elate sylvestris*, or wild date, and of these the soil is said to be saline.'

While travelling from Hosadurga towards Banavara, Buchanan came across extensive areas near Budihal where wild date or *Elate sylvestris* was very common (May 7, 1801). He also expressed the opinion that such an important tree resource could be more profitably utilized.

> "In every part of the *Budihalu* district the wild date (*Elate sylvestris*) is very common, but is of little use except for fuel. The present number of inhabitants cannot consume a hundredth part of the juice that could be extracted from it. This tree might be a source of considerable advantage, could a good spirit be extracted from its *Jagory*, of which I think there is little doubt; but from the wretched stills of the natives this can never be expected."

While travelling from Banavara towards Halebeedu, Buchanan passed through an area known as *Jamagullu* (Javagal - in Hassan district) where he had noticed that wild date (*Elate sylvestris*) had come up in areas which earlier were paddy fields that had been abandoned by the cultivators due to the wrath of invaders.

> "**May 11. Appearance of the country**. – I went three long cosses to *Jamagullu*. The country is rather more broken than that through which I have come for the last two days, and is equally deserted. The wild date has even over grown much of the rice-land. *Jamagullu* at present contains about eighty houses, and has a fort. Before the invasion of *Triumbaca Mama*, it was a large place, but has never since recovered."

Borassus flabellifer (palmyra palm/tale palm)

Buchanan described the Palmyra tree (*Borassus flabellifer*) in detail in the beginning of his journey much prior to entering the Mysore State, while passing through the countryside of the Madras Presidency (April 25, 1800). He also compared this species with another species *Elate sylvestris* (wild date). In India, the juice exuded by both these trees was traditionally used for making spirituous drink as well as jaggery.

> "The *Tari*, or fermented juice, and the *Jagory*, or inspissated juice of the *Palmira* tree (*Borassus flabelliformis*), are in this country more esteemed, than those of the wild date, which is contrary to the opinion of the *Bengalese*. The people of the *Carnatic* allege, that the produce of the latter is very heating. They pretend to be very moderate in the use of the *Tari*, but consume much of the *Jagory*. It sells in the country for 30 *Vees*, a *Pagoda*, or about 9*s*. 5*d*. a hundred-weight. Could it be converted into either a palatable spirituous liquor, or sugar, the barren plains of the *Carnatic* might be rendered productive. The former appears not to be improbable, and seems to be an object worth trying. If it should answer, the whole of the grain distilled in Europe might be saved for food."

It may be noted that Buchanan had made the above observations regarding the *Elate sylvestris*, or the wild date tree, prior to his arrival in the Mysore State. Apparently, before undertaking his journey, Buchanan had acquired sufficient information about the abundance as well as limited use of this tree in Mysore. In fact, as we have seen, during his journey through Mysore he came across this tree in many places whereas the Palmira (*Borassus*) was met with only on one occasion. The latter species was more common in the Madras Presidency.

While continuing to travel through the countryside of the Madras Presidency, Buchanan provided an account of the method of collection and processing of the juice of the *Palmira* tree (*Borassus flabellifer*) and the income derived from this activity, although he had suspected that the actual income from the produce was more than what was indicated to him.

"Palmira tree, or Borassus – The people, who make *Jogory* from palm trees, follow no other profession. An individual of this profession in the *Tamul* language is called *Shanan*, but collectively the cast is called *Shanar*. The *Shanan* mounts the *Palmira* tree morning and evening, in order to collect the exuded juice, which through the day he and his family boil down into *Jagory*. The tree produces at all seasons. One man can take care of 200 trees; from which, according to their account, he can extract annually 20 *Manugu*, or about 482 pounds of *Jagory*, worth at this place 6 *Pagodas*; which, at the usual exchange, is £2. 8s. or rather more than eleven shillings the cwt. Besides, the *Shanan* daily sells one or two *Fanams'* worth of *Tari*. According to this account, the produce of 200 *Palmira* trees would be

Jagory	*Pagodas*	6	0
Tari at 1½ *Fanam* daily-		15	7½
		21	7½
Deduct rent at 2 *Fanams* a tree		11	4
Profit	*Pagodas*	10	3½

I suspect, that by this account the produce is under-rated. If it were true, I can hardly see, how the *Shanan* could maintain a family in a country where provisions are by no means cheap."

In Mysore State, Buchanan came across the Palmira tree (*Borassus flabellifer*) near Channapatna (June 11, 1800) and commented in the following words.

"Palmira, or Borassus flabelliformis. - In this vicinity the *Palmira* tree thrives remarkably well, and is planted in barren dry spots, where the other palms will not succeed. It is only used for *Tari*, or wine, and that is never distilled, and seldom made into *Jagory*. Its stem is considered as much better for building than that of the coco-nut."

When travelling to Malabar, Buchanan had passed through the Kollegal areas, then under the Company's administration. He mentioned about the initiative taken by the district administration to plant *Borassus* (October 6, 1800).

> "**Palmira tree**. - Major Macleod, the collector, has just now sent up people with the seed of the *Palmira* tree, or *Borassus flabelliformis*, in order to instruct those here in the manner of cultivating that palm. They are forming a plantation on good land, a quarter of a coss in length, and 200 yards wide. The people here were formerly supplied with palm-wine from the wild date; but by the orders of the *Sultan* these were all cut; for the rigidity of this prince's morals would not allow him to permit, in his territory, the growth of an intoxicating substance."

OIL YIELDING TREES

In his travel diaries Buchanan described about the extraction of oil from the seed of a number of plant species that were cultivated as regular agricultural or horticultural crops. These included the sesamum (*Wull-Ellu*), niger (*Huts'-Ellu),* castor (*Harulu*), coco-nut (*Cobri*), etc. In addition, Buchanan provided information about a few trees or shrubs from the seed of which oil was extracted for lighting or other purposes.

Buchanan had given the following description about the plant *Jatropha curcas* (Mara haralu) which he had seen during his evening walk in the woods near Bidadi where he had camped on 13th May, 1800.

> "*2. Mara Haralu, Iatropha Curcas*, Lin. From the seed of this shrub, oil for the lamp is extracted, by the following process. Parch the seed in an earthen pot, then bruise it, and put the powder in boiling water for three hours. The oil then rises to the surface, and is removed by skimming. This oil being much used by the poor, the plant is frequently raised in the hedges near villages; but it is also found wild in almost every copse, especially near the banks of torrents." [**Note**: Buchanan had used the word *Iatropha* instead of *Jatropha*.]

Buchanan was given a specimen of the same plant from the forests of *Savana-durga* in Magadi (June 15-19, 1800) and he described it as follows:

> *"Mara Haralu, Jatropa curcas.* Its seed is collected for lamp oil. The dried stems answer excellently for match, as they burn slowly, and without flame."

During his second visit to Bangalore where he had camped from 22nd June to 2nd July, 1800, Buchanan had ascertained the following information about extraction of oil from the seed of *Bassia longifolia* (ippe) and *Robinia mitis* (*Pongamia pinnata* - honge).

> **"Ipay, or Bassia oil. –** The *Ipay* oil, made from the fruit of *Bassia longifolia,* is used for the lamps burned before the gods, being esteemed of a better quality than that of the *Ricinus.* The mill takes 70 *Seers* measure, and the seed requires to be moistened with 12 *Cucha Seers* (3½ ale quarts) of tamarind water, in which 2 *Seers* of tamarinds have been infused. The produce is 70 *Seers* (4 365/1000 ale gallons) of oil. The cake is used as soap to wash oil out of the hair of those who anoint themselves."

> **"Hoingay oil.** – The *Hoingay* oil, produced from the seed of the *Robinia mitis,* is used for the lamp; but it consumes very quickly. It is also used externally in many diseases. Take 70 Seers, *Pucca* measure, of the seed freed from the pods, add 4 *Cucha Seers* measure of water (1 11/100 ale quart), and beat them in a mortar into a paste. Then tread the paste with the feet; and, having kept it for two or three days, dry it in the sun. It is then put into the mill with one *Cucha* Seer (19 6/10 cubical inches) of water. It produces 40 Seers (2¾ ale gallons) of oil. For fewel, the cake is mixed with cow-dung."

Neem oil

Although Buchanan mentioned about the presence of the *Melia azadirachta* (*Bewu*) tree in the forests of *Savana-durga* in Magadi, he did not refer to its oil-bearing property. Earlier, while travelling through the Madras territories (April 25, 1800), he had indicated that oil was extracted from the seeds of the tree in the district surrounding Madras.

> "*Vaypa any*, oil of the seeds of the *Melia azadirachta*. About an ounce of this is given to every woman, immediately after she is delivered of a child. It is used also for the lamp."

Oil from seed of *Calophyllum inophyllum* (undimara)

Buchanan had also mentioned (February 25, 1801) about the extraction of oil in the coastal region of Canara from the seeds of *Calophyllum inophyllum* tree.

> "**Feb. 20. Poon, or Puna, the Inophyllum of Linnaeus**. – I went three cosses to *Beiluru*, which signifies the *cleared place*, and is a common name in countries where the dialect of *Karnata* prevails. My tents were, however, pitched in a very stately grove of the **Calophyllum inophyllum**, which in this part of the country is much planted near the villages. It grows to a large size, especially in sandy places near the sea. The common lamp oil of the country is expressed from its seed, by means of a mill turned by oxen. It is here called *Hoingay*, the name by which above the *Ghats* the *Robinia mitis* is known. In *Tulava* and *Malayala* it is called *Puna*, by us commonly written *Poon*. I suspect that the *Poon* of the eastern islands is different."

> [**Note:** *Tulava* refers to the southern part of Canara where the principal language spoken was *Tulu*. The northern limits of the *Tulava* region extended up to Baindur, i.e. up to south of Bhatkal.]

GUM YIELDING TREES

Buchanan had mentioned about a number of trees yielding gum/resin that he had come across during his travel in Mysore and Canara.

Present scientific and local names	Local and scientific names used by Buchanan	Comments of Buchanan
Chloroxylon swietenia (Dhoopa)	*Chadacalu, Chloroxylon Dupada*, Buch. MSS.	An elegant tree, producing a resin that is frequently used in the temples, as incense.
Soymida febrifuga (Some)	*Swamy, Swietenia febrifuga*, Roxb. MSS.	A strong, but small tree, produces a fine clear gum.
Anogeissus latifolia (Dindiga/ Dindal)	*Dinduga, Andersonia Panchamoum*, Roxb. MSS.	A large valuable timber tree, that is used for planks, beams, pillars, and furniture. It abounds in gum, and is nearly allied to the *Conocarpus* of botanists.
Melia azadirachta (Bevu/Neem)	*Bewu, Melia azadirachta.*	A large timber tree, that is much used here, and from which a gum exudes.
Buchanania lanzan (Nurkal/ Murkal)	*Muruculu, Chirongia glabra*, Buch. MSS.	In many parts, and especially near *Chinapatam*, this is the most common tree. Its wood is not much valued; but it produces large quantities of dark-coloured gum. The fruit is esculent.

While passing through Ramanagara (*Rama-giri*) on 12th June, 1800, Buchanan had elicited the following information about a number of gums obtained from trees/plants; collection of these gums was done by a hill tribe known as *Chensu* (*Cad' Eriligaru*, or *Cat' Chensu*).

"When ordered, the *Chensu* collect gum from various trees; but they never do it without a special commission, and the quantity that they could procure is inconsiderable. The trees which produce it are,

Dinduga,	-	*Andersonia Panshomoum,* Rox. MSS.
Bewu,		*Melia azadirachta.*
Muruculu,	-	*Chirongia glabra,* Buch. MSS.
Mavena,	-	*Mangifera Indica.*
Avaricai,	-	*Cassia auriculata.*
Nugay,		
Bayla,	-	*Aegle marmelos.*
Jala,	-	*Shorea Jala,* Buch. MSS.
Chadacalu,	-	*Chloroxylon Dupada,* Buch. MSS.
Betta Tovary,	-	*Bombax gossypinum,* Lin."

Buchanan also mentioned of a sticky substance (glue) called *Chunderasu* which was used as size for false gilding (a process by which shiny gold-colored paper cuttings with floral designs were pasted on to the walls and columns of the palaces at Srirangapatna for ornamental purpose.) The *Chunderasu* was also used in painting work.

"The *Chunderasu* is prepared from the milky juice of any of the following trees: (*Ficus glomerata* Roxb.), *Goni* (a tree which I call *Ficus gonia*), *Bayala, Bayvina, Gobali,* &c. It is therefore an elastic gum."

"The oil used for painting consists of two parts of linseed, and one part of *Chunderasu.*"

[**Note:** The species mentioned are *Ficus glomerata* (atti), *Ficus mysorensis* (goni), *Aegle marmelos* (bael/bilva), bevu (*Azadirachta indica*) and *Acacia nilotica* (karijali/gobli). Buchanan Vol. I; Page 75.]

TREES/PLANTS YIELDING CORDAGE (ROPES)

Among the trees found in forest, Buchanan mentioned about two trees bark of which yields ropes. These were as follows:

Present scientific and local names	Local and scientific names used by Buchanan	Comments of Buchanan
Cordia monoica (Panugeri)	*Narwully, Cordia monoica*, Roxb.	Ropes are made of its bark. The fruit is esculent, but tasteless.
Eriolaena quinquelocularis (Goomchi/Gomajjige/ Kondigida/ Katale)	*Gumshia. Gumsia chloroxylon* Buch. MSS.	It does not grow to a large size; but the timber is said to be very strong, and has a singular green colour. Ropes are made of its bark.

In addition, Buchanan mentioned about another three species which were used for making ropes. While travelling from Bethamangala to Tekal (*Tayculum*) on 6th May, 1800, Buchanan had mentioned about the local people making cordage from the leaves of the plant *Agave vivipara* (aloe) which they had grown in their hedges. He also mentioned (June 3, 1801) about the preparation of cordage for the military stores at Srirangapatna from the leaves of the same plant.

While travelling from Tavarekere to Bangalore on 21st June, 1800, Buchanan gave the following description of a plant species called *Aletris nervosus*.

"*Aletris nervosus.* – The leaves of the *Aletris nervosus*, Roxb: are used here for making cordage. Before they are beaten to separate the fibres, they are steeped in water fifteen days, in order to rot the useless parts."

When camping at Bangalore during the period from June 22 to July 2, 1800, Buchanan had given a detailed description about the cultivation of the species *Crotalaria juncea* (*Janupa*) which was the main source of *Goni*, a coarse, but very strong sack-cloth, an important article of manufacture.

TREES AND PLANTS YIELDING DYES

While passing through Ramanagara (*Rama-giri*) on 12th June, 1800, Buchanan had also obtained information about a number of dyes sourced from trees/plants, and which were collected and supplied by the *Chensu* tribe.

> "----*Popli*, a bark used as a red dye. The plant that produces it is a scandent shrub, the flower of which I could never find; nor did Dr. Roxburgh know it by the dry specimen of the branches in leaf. It seems, however, to be nearly related to the *Ventilago*. The *Muddi*, or the bark of the root of at least two kinds of *Morinda*, is also used as a dye; as is likewise the *Capily Podi*. It is the red dust shaken from the fruit of *Rotleria tinctoria*. The merchants of *Bangaluru* and *Colar* buy up these articles, paying to the *Chensu* a *Fanam* for 32 *Seers* of *Popli*, and *Muddy*, or 3*s*. 10½*d*. a hundred weight, and a *Fanam* for one *Seer* of *Capily Podi*, or 1*s*. 1 ¼ *d*. a pound.

> [**Note**: *Rotleria tinctoria* is now known as *Wrightia tinctoria* (hale/beppale).]

While travelling from Madhugiri towards Thovenakere (August 12, 1800), Buchanan had come across a forest harboring the plant that yielded the *Popli Podi* dye. He gave the following description.

> "**Popli bark**. - In the neighbouring woods is found abundance of the *Popli* bark, which I have frequently mentioned as a dye, and as an article of export. It is the bark of the root of a large scandent plant, which climbs to the top of the highest trees. I saw neither flower nor fruit, so I can say nothing of its botanical affinities; and the specimens of the stem and leaves were not known to Dr. Roxburgh. It is collected by some *Baydarus*, who are in the service of the *Gydda Cavila*, or keeper of the forest."

While travelling past *Manday Gudday* (Mandagadde) (April 1, 1801), Buchanan had seen trees of *Cedrela toona* the flowers of which were used to make a dye. He gave the following description.

> "***Tundu* flowers, a dye**. - Near the town, I observed many fine trees of the *Tundu*, or *Cedrela Tuna* Roxb: MSS. Its flowers, as I have mentioned at *Bangalore*, are used for dying. It is said, that they are collected by Mussulmans, who gather them every morning as they fall from the tree, and afterwards dry them on mats exposed to the sun. The price at present is said to be so low, that none are collected."

MYROBALANS

Although the forests harbored a number of species which came under the group of myrobalans, fruit of *Terminalia chebula* (alalekai) was the most important and widely used myrobalan in the tanning industry of the Mysore State. It was also used for dyeing.

TREES/PLANTS YIELDING DRUGS/MEDICINES

When travelling near Ramanagara (*Rama-giri*) (June 12, 1800), Buchanan had been informed that the *Chensu* tribesmen collect two types of drug from the forest, namely, *Agulusunti* and *Hegguntigay*. Further details about the drugs were not provided.

During his stay at Bangalore (June 22 to July 2, 1800), Buchanan had obtained information about various drugs and their collection, trade etc. His observations are reproduced below.

> "**Drugs.** – A kind of drug merchants at *Bangalore*, called *Gandhaki*, trade to a considerable extent. Some of them are *Banijigaru*, and others are *Ladaru*, a kind of Mussulmans. They procure the medicinal plants of the country by means of a set of people called *Pacanat Jogalu*, who have huts in the woods, and, for leave to collect the drugs, pay a small rent to the *Gaudas* of the villages. They bring the drugs hither in small caravans of ten or twelve oxen, and sell

them to the *Gandhaki*, who retail them. None of them are exported. Small traders from neighbouring towns bring *Popli* and *Muddi* barks; honey, and wax; *Agalasunti*, and *Hayguntigay*, two medicinal roots, *Myrobalans*, and *Dinduga* gum; all of which they procure from the *Eriligaru*. The whole wax of the country used formerly to be brought hither; but now a great part of it is carried directly to the lower *Carnatic*. The quantity annually procured does not exceed a hundred *Maunds*, or about 2,425 pounds. The *Dinduga* gum might be had to the extent of two or three hundred *Maunds*, or from 4,850 lbs. to 7,275 lbs. a year, if money were advanced for it at the rate of from 8 to 12 *Fanams* a *Maund*, or from 1*l.* 3*s.* 4*d.* to 1*l.* 15*s.* 1*d.* the hundred weight. At present a small quantity only is collected for the use of the silk-weavers. The cotton-merchants from the *Duab* of the *Krishna* supply the *Gandhaki* with *Cut*, or terra japonica; with asafoetida; *Mailtuta* and *Maiful*, two substances used by the natives in cleaning their teeth; *Costa*, a medicine; *Loduchica*, a dye; sulphur; alum; borax; and opium. From the *Gandhaki* these merchants purchase *Muddi* and *Popli* dyes; *lac*, and wax. The *lac* is partly bought from the *Woddar*, who collect it in the neighbourhood; and partly from traders, that bring it from *Madhu-giri*, *Godagiri*, *Bannirgutta*, and *Denkina-cotay*. The spices, the *Tagashay* seed, and indigo, are procured by the *Gandhaki* from the lower *Carnatic*. Fossile alkali, or soda, is partly brought from *Krishna-giri* in the *Bara-mahal*; and partly from *Chin-raya-pattana*, *Gutalu*, and Holy *Nara-singa-pura*. *Tonda* flowers, for dyeing, are brought from *Nagara*, and from *Denkina-cotay*; those produced in the latter place are the best. Most of the *Capili-podi* dye, or flower produced on the fruit of the *Rotleria tinctoria* of Dr. Roxburgh, comes from *Chin-raya-pattana*; but a little is procured from *Rama-giri*. The *Cossumba*, or *Carthamus tinctorius*, that grows in the country, is not nearly sufficient for its demand; and much of this article is imported by the cotton-merchants from the Duab."

[**Note:** It may be noted that collection and trading of drugs and other products including dyeing agents were done together.]

While describing the commercial fair at Gubbi (September 15, 1800), Buchanan mentioned about a weekly fair held at Birur, where the plant called *Bagy*, or *Calamus aromaticus* (Baje) was bought by the merchants of *Nagara* and of *Malayala* from the merchants of Gubbi. Although the properties of this species had not been mentioned by Buchanan, it apparently was for medicinal purposes.

FOOD AND RELATED PRODUCTS FROM FOREST

Buchanan mentioned about a number of trees which provided edible fruits or seeds. These included *Tari, Myrobalanus Taria,* Buch. MSS. (kernel); *Muruculu, Chironjia glabra,* Buch. MSS. (kernel); *Nelli, Phyllanthus emblica,* (fruit); *Wontay, Artocarpus Bengalensis* Roxb: MSS (fruit).

Honey and wax were two important products from the forest. Usually these two items were collected from the forest by the forest-dwelling tribal people who supplied these to the people living outside the forests. With regard to collection of honey and wax by the *Chensu* tribe living near Ramanagara (*Rama-giri*), Buchanan described as follows (June 12, 1800):

> "The *Chensu* here live upon game, wild roots, herbs, and fruits; and a little grain, which they purchase from the farmers. They are enabled to do this by collecting some drugs, honey, and wax. It is on account of their having the exclusive privilege of collecting these two last articles, that they pay a poll-tax, which is annually fifteen *Fanams,* or 10*s.* 0 ¾*d.* for each family.

> "**Bees.** – The bees are of two kinds: one, smaller than our bee, builds its nest on the twigs of trees, and is easily procured; the other is a large bee, which builds in the clefts of rocks, and its honey is obtained with great difficulty. The wax sells at 2½ *Seers* for the *Fanam* or 1*l.* 8s. 4*d.* a hundred weight. The honey sells at 2 *Seers* for the *Fanam.*"

Regarding other food articles collected and supplied by the *Chensu* tribe, Buchanan wrote as follows:

"The principal articles of vegetable food collected by the *Chensu*, are, the seed of the *Bamboo*, and several kinds of *Dioscorea*, or Yams, that grow wild in the neighbouring woods."

During his halt at Madhugiri (July 25-29, 1800), Buchanan provided further information about bees found in the forest and also about the method of collection of honey and wax.

"**Bees.** – The bees here are of four kinds: **I.** That from which most of the honey and wax is procured, is called *Hegenu*. This is a large bee, which builds under projections of the rocks, or in caverns. A large nest gives *8 Seers, Seringapatam* weight, of honey = 4 85/100 lb. and 3 *Seers* of wax 1 82/100 lb. A small hive gives about one third of this quantity. The honey is gathered twice a year, in *Ashadha* and *Magha*, or in the month following the summer solstice, and the second after that of winter. Some people of the *Baydaru* cast make the collecting of honey and wax a profession, and it is one attended with much danger. Having discovered a hive, some of them kindle a fire under the rock, and throw on it the leaves of the *Cassia fistula*, and of the *Puleseri*, which emit a smoke so acrid, that nothing living can endure it. The bees are forced to retire; and some others of the *Baydas*, so soon as the smoke subsides, lower down by a rope one of their companions, who with a pole knocks off the nest, and is immediately drawn up again; for, if he made any delay, the bees would return, and their stinging is so violent, that it endangers life. In order to fortify him against the sharp points of rocks, and against injury from the rope, which passes round his chest, the adventurous *Bayda* is secured, before and behind, by several folds of leather. **II.** The bee, that produces the next greatest quantity of honey is called the *Cadi*, or *Chittu Jainu*, that is, stick, or small honey. This bee is very small, and builds, around the branch of a tree, a comb of an oblong shape, and sharpened at both ends. It is found at all seasons, but is in the greatest perfection at the same time with the other. The honey is of the finest quality; but the whole comb seldom weighs more than two *Seers*, or 1 2/10 lb. This bee does not sting, and is readily driven away by a twig switched round the comb. **III.** The *Tuduvay* is a bee of which the honey is of an excellent quality, but rarely procured; for it generally builds deep in the crevices of rocks, where it is totally inaccessible. Sometimes, however, it is found in hollow trees, and one hive will give from 20 to 25 *Seers* of honey, or about 12 to 15 pounds; but the quantity of wax is in proportion small. This is a large bee, but it very seldom stings those who plunder its hive. **IV.** The *Togriga* is a very small bee, that seldom stings. It takes possession of the deserted nests of the white ants (*Termes*), which in this country are very numerous in the wastes of red soil, such as is usually cultivated for *Ragy*. Of this stiff earth, the white ants raise hills resembling the stump of a tree, which are from four to six feet high, very hard, and able long to resist the heaviest rain. These, when deserted, most commonly become the lurking places of snakes; but sometimes give shelter to the *Togriga* bee. Its nest is therefore easily accessible; but it is very small, and contains only about a *Seer* of honey, and half a *Seer* of wax."

[**Note**: *Puleseri* is the local (Telugu) name of the species *Schleichera trijuga/oleosa*.]

While touring through Canara, Buchanan had noticed that pepper vines (*Piper nigrum*) occurred naturally in the moister valleys within the forests and the local inhabitants, after carrying out partial thinning of trees and manipulation of the canopy, tied the wild vines to trees thereby assisting the vines to climb up. These vines in due course of time produce luxuriant crop of black pepper. In fact, black pepper was one of the primary products of the region. [Farming of pepper will be discussed further in *Chapter 6.*]

In addition to pepper, two other important products of the forests of Canara were Nutmeg (including mace) and Cinnamon. While passing through the forests near *Mirzee* on 25th February, 1801, Buchanan wrote the following in respect of these two forest products.

"**Nutmeg**. - The wild nutmeg and *Cassia* are very common. As the nutmegs ripen, the monkeys always eat up the outer rind, and mace; so that I could not procure one in a perfect state. They are collected from the ground, after having been peeled by the monkeys, and are sold by some poor people to the shopkeepers; but they have little flavour; and the demand for them is very small. Although they are, doubtless, of a distinct species, from the nutmeg of *Amboyna*, it is probable, that by proper cultivation and manure their quality might be greatly improved; and that, in the situations where they now grow spontaneously, they might be reared as the supporters of the pepper vine; which would produce copiously, and of an excellent quality, were the same pains bestowed on it here as is done in the gardens above the *Ghats*, where by far the best pepper grows."

"***Laurus Cassia***. - The *Cassia* belongs to government, and is in general given in lease; but at present no renter can be procured. Its quality also might, no doubt, be greatly improved; and by cutting the shoots, when of a proper size, and cleaning and rolling up the bark neatly, it might be made equal to the *Cassia* of *China*."

With regard to the nutmeg tree, what Buchanan came across in Canara was perhaps the species *Myristica dactyloides/beddomi* (jayaphal/jajikai) or *Myristica malabarica* (dodda jajikai). The improved variety of nutmeg he was referring to is the species *Myristica fragrans*, which is a native of Indonesia (*Amboyna*). Buchanan's vision of improving the quality of the spice more than 200 years ago became a reality, as it is the species *Myristica fragrans* which the people of the *malnad* region of Karnataka have been cultivating in their gardens.

FOREST TRIBES AND SUPPLY OF FOREST PRODUCTS

It has been mentioned that the *Chensu* tribe had played an important role in forest areas around Ramanagara in collecting drugs, dyes, food articles, etc. from forest and then supplying these to the consumers. Buchanan had mentioned about a few more tribes who had performed similar role in other parts of Mysore. While touring near Periyapatna (September 11-13, 1800), Buchanan collected the following information regarding trading of forest products with the forest tribes.

"There is at present no *Gyda Cavila*, or forest-renter; but formerly there used to be one, who, having made friendship with the wild tribes called *Cad' Eravaru*, and *Jain Curubaru*, procured from them honey and wax, *Popli chica*, a dye, *Dupada* wood, *Gunti Beru*, a root used in dyeing, *Cad' Arsina*, or wild turmeric, and *Cadu Baly Aly*, or the leaves of the wild plantain tree, which are used by the natives as dishes. For timber, or grass, no rent was demanded."

Buchanan came across another tribe known as *Soligaru* who lived in the forests of Kollegala. With regard to their trade with the farmers, Buchanan wrote the following (October 7, 1800).

"-----The men supply the farmers with timber and *Bamboos*; and they gather various esculent leaves, and wild *Yams*. They also collect honey, which they immediately eat.---"

MARKET PRICES OF FOREST PRODUCTS

During his stay at Bangalore from June 22 to July 2, 1800, Buchanan had made enquiries and ascertained the average prices of the principal goods sold at Bangalore market. The prices of various goods sourced from forest as ascertained and described by Buchanan are given in the following table. Sandalwood has not been included in this table, as it has already been discussed in *Chapter 2*.

| Kind of goods. | Quality. | Sultany Fanams. | | English money. Cwt. |
		Maund.	Cwt.	£. s. d.
Arulay, or *Myrobalans*	----	1½	6½	0 4 4½
Cut, or *Terra Japonica*	White	16	69½	2 6 8
	Red	14	60 8/10	2 0 10
	Black	12	52 1/8	1 15 1
Tundu flowers	Nagara	10	43 4/10	1 9 2
	Denkina cotay	17	73 8/10	2 9 7

Nutmegs		200	868	29 11 4
Mace		1720	7471½	250 1 9¼
Shicai fruit		1	4 1/3	0 2 11¼
Popli-chica dye		6	26 1/16	0 17 6½
Lodu-chica dye		25	108½	3 12 11
Honey		6	26 1/16	0 17 6½
Bees-wax	Yellow	30	130 5/10	4 7 8½
Stick-*lac*	Cleaned	14	60 8/10	2 0 10
	Including the sticks	6	26 1/16	0 17 6½
Muddi-chica dye		6	26 1/16	0 17 6½
Dinduga gum	1ˢᵗ sort	8	34¾	1 3 4
	2ⁿᵈ sort	6	26 1/16	0 17 6½
Capily-podi a dye	*Rama-giri*	70	304 1/16	10 4 4½
	Nagara	40	170¾	5 16 8
Black pepper		16	73¾	2 9 7¼

(**Note**: One *Maund* is equal to 42½ *Seers*, except for black pepper for which one *Maund* is equal to 40 *Seers*)

Towards the end of his tour in Canara, Buchanan had received from Mr. Read, the collector of the northern division of Canara, a detailed report regarding the production of various commodities in the northern division. In respect of forest produce, Mr. Read had used the words 'The produce of the wastelands brought to market', as the concept of forest land as an administrative entity had not yet evolved. Mr. Read provided the following information about the annual production of forest produces (other than sandalwood, teak and rosewood*).

	Annual produce of honey.	Annual produce of bees wax.	Annual produce wild cinnamon.	Annual produce of Cabob China.	Annual produce nutmegs.	Annual produce of wild pepper.
	Maunds.	*Maunds.*	*Maunds.*	*Maunds.*	*Maunds.*	*Maunds.*
Kundapura	-	-	8 30	25 30	-	51 0
Honawera	-	-	99 35	42 32½	12 5	533 0
Ancola	8 0	2 7½	15 10	50 14	28 17½	474 38¾
Supa	33 23	49 6	15 30	5 10	-	-
Soonda, or Sudha	8 7	29 28½	2 0	1 0	-	-
Banawasi	11 24	3 13	-	-	-	-
Billighy	-	-	-	43 0	-	34 8

[**Note:** One *Maund* weighs 24 84/100 lb. and is divided into 40 *Seers.*]

(* Details regarding sandalwood production have been given in *Chapter 2* and those regarding teak and rosewood have been given in *Chapter 3*)

Buchanan had noted that the above table had not included the production of *Cut,* or *Terra Japonica.* He commented thus: 'The *Cut,* and perhaps some other articles of less importance, have eluded Mr. Read's enquiries, probably from their never having been objects of revenue.' Buchanan had also observed that although wild pepper was collected at *Soonda Taluc,* it had not been reported to Mr. Read.

Chapter 6

TREES IN FARMLANDS

During his visit to various parts of Mysore and Canara, Buchanan had keenly observed and made enquiries about the agricultural operations associated with different crops grown in the farmlands. In his writings, he described these operations in minute detail. Having recognized the beneficial effects of trees on agriculture, Buchanan made it a point to mention the various practical ways through which farmers had made use of trees and other plants in order to enhance farm productivity. In particular, he mentioned how farmers increased the soil fertility and soil moisture by using the leaves of various trees, shrubs and herbs as manure or mulch. He mentioned about the different trees that were planted as nurse crop or as support to climbers such as pepper vine and betel vine. He also wrote in detail about the trees and shrubs that the farmers had planted along the boundaries of their farmlands in order to retain moisture and also to ward off intruders including animals.

CASSIA FISTULA (KAKKE) – FAVOURITE OF *VIGNESHA*

"Cacay, Cassia fistula, Lin. This is the greatest ornament of the woods of *Karnata*. The foliage is a fine shining green; and the pendulous strings of flowers surpass those of the *Laburnum*, not only in beauty, but in length and number. In the cool of the morning they diffuse a most agreeable perfume. The plant is sacred to *Ganeswara*, the god that is addressed by all those who are about to commence any undertaking; as he is considered to be the Power that hinders or stops all human efforts, in the same manner as his father *Iswara* is the Power that deprives all beings of life. The people here, instead of addressing themselves immediately to the god, worship him under the form of his favourite tree. At this season, the cultivators of every village place a stake of the *Cacay* in the ground, level a circular space around it, and purify this area with cow-dung. On this spot they assemble before the commencement of seed-time, burn some incense before the stake, make offerings of rice, milk, and the like, and pray that it will not prevent the success of their crops. The ceremony concludes with a rural feast." (Buchanan, Vol. I. Page Nos. 51-52)

The above narration by Buchanan is indicative of an intrinsic bond between farmers and nature. This bond was not merely symbolic or ritualistic, as the *Meity*, or priest to the stake of *Cacay*, or *Cassia fistula*, was traditionally entitled to a share of the crop produced in the land. (Buchanan. Vol. II. Page No. 109)

TREES AS MANURE OR MULCH

Before starting his tour to various parts of Mysore and Canara, Buchanan had camped at Srirangapatna for a number of days (May 17 to June 5, 1800). During that period he paid a visit to Mysore and went around the countryside in the vicinity of Srirangapatna, acquiring information about various aspects including people, their livelihoods and lifestyles, administration, agriculture, livestock, trade and commerce, arts, etc. 'From the 20th of May, to the 5th of June, I was employed in visiting everything remarkable in *Seringapatam* and its neighbourhood, and in taking an account of the state of agriculture, arts, and commerce at that place.' Buchanan had devoted a lot of his time with rapt attention to see and learn about the agricultural practices adopted in the region. A considerable part of his diaries written during his stay in Srirangapatna centered on agriculture and related activities of that period. His observations with regard to manuring of soil are contained in the following paragraph.

"**Manures.** - A good deal of attention is here paid to manuring the soil. Every farmer has a dunghill; which is prepared by digging a pit of sufficient extent; in this is collected the whole of the dung and litter of the cattle from the houses where they are kept, together with all the ashes and soil of the family. The straw, and various leaves intended to be used as manure, are never mixed with the dung. The farmers, who are within two miles of the city, send bullocks with sacks, and procure from the *Halal*, or sweepers, the ashes, ordure, and other soil of the town. This also is kept separate from the dunghill. The straws of various crops, as before-mentioned, are reserved for manure, and to these are added various leaves of wild plants; the *Cogay Sopu*, or *Galega purpurea*; the *Hoingay Sopu*, or *Robinia mitis*; the *Tumbay Sopu*, or *Phlomis esculenta* of Dr. Roxburgh's MSS.; the *Ugany Sopu*, a *Convolvulus*: the *Atty Sopu*, or *Ficus glomerata*, R.; the *Umutty Sopu*, or *Datura metel*; and *Yeccada Sopu*, or *Asclepias gigantea*. These leaves, and the straw, are the manure given to rice ground in the *sprouted-seed* and *transplanted* cultivations. When the field has been reduced to mud, a sufficient quantity of the manure is trampled into the puddle, and, with the moisture and heat of this climate, soon rots. The dung in every part of *Mysore* is most commonly carried on carts, which are applied to scarcely any other purpose. The city-soil is reckoned best for sugar-cane, but is also given to various grains. The use of lime as a manure is totally unknown to the natives; who, indeed, consider all ground, naturally impregnated with that substance, as very unfit for most kinds of cultivation. This accords well enough with the theory of Lord Dundonald, who supposes that lime is useful by promoting the putrefaction of inert vegetable matter. The heat of the climate is here sufficient for the purpose; and the lime, which in a cold climate may be necessary, would be here destructive, by exhausting the vegetable matter too quickly."

[**Note:** The present name of *Galega purpurea* is *Tephrosia purpurea* (koggili/empali/punike/marali/sharpapunkhi); *Asclepias gigantea* is now known as *Calotropis gigantea* (ekke)]

Buchanan mentioned about the use of a mixture of cow-dung and fresh plants of *Tumbay Sopu*, or *Phlomis esculenta* (present name *Leucas aspera*) in the rice (paddy) fields near Mandya (June 7, 1800).

During his tour in the vicinity of Maddur (June 8, 1800), Buchanan had mentioned about the use of *Euphorbium tirucalli* as manure for saline soil.

> "**Saline earth**. - In this part of the country much of the soil is impregnated with saline matter, and called *Soulu munnu*. Of this there are two kinds; one chiefly impregnated with carbonate of soda, the other with the muriates of soda and magnesia. The latter would produce nothing: the former is cultivated, although it produces poor crops. The manure used for it is formed of the branches of the *Euphorbium Tirucalli*, which in this part of the country are never used on any other kind of rice-ground. In the country near *Madras* they are, for all soils, the most esteemed manure."

While touring in the neighbourhood of Ramanagara (*Rama-giri*), Buchanan had remarked that the practice of littering the cowsheds with straw was not practiced by all the farmers (June 12, 1800).

> "The cows are always kept in a house at night, and by some are littered with straw; but by others this is neglected.---"

> [**Note**: Littering of the cowshed with straw, grass or leaves was a very healthy practice that was adopted by farmers in various parts of Mysore and Canara. It was an important organic way of augmenting the quantity of manure required for improving the fertility and water holding capacity of the soil.]

Buchanan was in Kolar between 8th and 11th July, 1800, when he studied the agricultural practices in this part of Mysore. His observations regarding the use of manure in this region were as follows:

> "**Manure**. - The leaves or shoots used by the farmers here as manure are, the *Handur*, the *Canaga*, or *Robinia mitis*, the *Yecada*, or

Asclepias gigantea; the *Calli,* or *Euphorbium Tirucalli;* the *Devadarum,* or *Erythroxylon sideroxyloides,* E. M.; the *Cadangody,* or *Convolvulvus cuneiformis,* Buch: MSS.; the *Gandary,* the *Utrany,* or *Achyranthes muricata;* the *Dotury,* or *Argemone;* the *Wumutty,* or *Datura Metel;* the *Tumbay,* or *Phlomis esculenta,* Dr. Roxburgh's MSS.; and the *Hangara,* or *Dodonea viscosa.*"

Buchanan further added the following.

"The farmers form their dung-hills of the dung and litter of their cattle, and of the ashes and soil of their houses, all intermixed. They do not employ the soil of the towns."

During the period from 25th to 29th July, 1800, Buchanan camped at Madhugiri and surveyed 'the country north from the *Ghats* of *Nandi-durga*'. While describing the method of rice cultivation in this part of the Mysore State, Buchanan provided the following information as to how the seed was prepared for sowing.

"July 25, &c. Manner of preparing the seed. - The only manner of cultivating rice, that is in use here, is the *Mola,* or sprouted-seed; the manner of preparing which is as follows. The ears must be cut off, the grain beat out immediately, and then dried in the sun three or four days. It must be preserved in straw or in jars. When wanted for sowing, it must be exposed to the sun for a day, and soaked in water all the following night. It is then put upon a layer of the leaves of the *Yecada,* or *Asclepias gigantea,* or of the *Harulu, Ricinus Palma Christi,* mixed with sheeps dung, and is surrounded by stones, so as to keep it together. It is then covered with *Bandury* leaves (*Dodonea Viscosa* Willd:) and pressed down with a stone. Next morning the upper leaves are removed, and a pot of water is thrown on the seed, which must be turned with the hand, and then covered again with the leaves and stone. Daily, for three or four times, this operation must be repeated, and then the sprouts from the seed will be almost an inch long."

[**Note**: The present name of *Ricinus Palma Christi* is *Ricinus communis* (castor/harulu)]

With regard to manure applied by the farmers to their farmlands in the neighbourhood of Madhugiri, Buchanan wrote as follows:

"**July 25, &c. Manure of leaves.** – The leaves used here as a manure for rice-land are those of the *Coghi*, or *Galega purpurea*; of the *Haingay*, or *Robinia mitis*; of the *Yecada*, or *Asclepias gigantea*; of the *Devadarum*, or *Erythroxylon sideroxyloides*, E. M.; of the *Calli*, or *Euphorbium Tirucalli*; and of the *Hut's Ellu*, a plant not yet described."

[**Note:** The plant *Hut's Ellu* was later identified by Buchanan as *Verbesina sativa* (Hucchellu/Uchellu/Niger or Black seed).]

Buchanan mentioned about the application of manure 'with equal parts of dung, and of mud from the bottoms of tanks, mixed with leaves of the *Robinia mitis*' in the cultivation of *Bili Jola*. He also mentioned about the use of the leaves of the *Robinia mitis* in the cultivation of sugar-cane: 'Near each cane, as a manure, some leaves of the *Robinia mitis* are then placed, and they are covered with a little mud;'

Regarding manuring of Areca-nut gardens in the vicinity of Madhugiri, Buchanan mentioned as follows:

"One year it is manured with dung; in the second with the leaves of the *Hoingay*, and *Coghi* (*Robinia mitis* and *Galega purpurea*), and in the third year with mud from the bottom of a reservoir. So long as the garden lasts, this succession of manures should, if possible, be continued;"

From 1st to 6th August, 1800, Buchanan 'remained at Sira investigating the state of the neighbourhood'. With regard to use of manure in the rice fields in this part of the country, Buchanan provided the following information.

"**Leaves used as manure**. – The leaves that are here used as manure for rice lands are, the *Hoingay*, or *Robinia mitis*; the *Coghi*, or *Galega purpurea*; the *Yecada*, or *Asclepias gigantea*; the *Tumbay*, or *Phlomis esculenta*, Dr. Roxburgh's MSS.; the *Womuttay*, or *Datura metel*; the *Calli*, or *Euphorbium Tirucalli*; and the *Hughinay*."

While narrating the method of rice-cultivation in the farmlands around Periyapatna, where he had camped during the period from 11th to 13th September, 1800, Buchanan narrated the following about the use of leaves as manure.

"**Sept. 11-13. Leaves used for manure.** – After the last ploughing, manure with the leaves of the *Chandra maligy* (*Mirabilis*), or *Womuttay* (*Datura metel*); but, if these cannot be had, with the leaves of *Chaudingy* (*Solanum*, not yet described, but which nearly resembles the *Verbascifolium*). Then tread the leaves into the mud, sow the seed very thick, and cover it with dung."

During his stay at Mangalore from 22nd to 29th January, 1801, Buchanan collected the following information regarding preparation of manure in the *Tulava* region.

"**Manure.** - The leaves of every kind of tree and bush, except such as are prickly, are used for manure. The cattle are kept in the house all night, and their dung is collected for the same use. It is kept in pits, and every day's collection is covered with leaves; the whole dunghill thus forming alternate strata of dung and leaves, which soon rot. The ashes and sweepings of the family are kept in a separate pit. The soil of towns is never used as manure."

While travelling through Karkala in Canara (February 8, 1801), Buchanan mentioned about use of the small branches and leaves of *Strychnos nux-vomica* (*Casara sopu*) as manure in the kitchen gardens in which turmeric, ginger, etc. were grown.

While camping at Haldipur (February 23, 1801) located in the *Haiga* country (occupied by the *Havikas*) in Canara, Buchanan had collected information about various types of manure used in this part of the country. His observations are reproduced below.

> **"Manure.** – At night the cattle in every part of *Haiga* are kept in the house, where they are daily well littered with fresh materials. The litter and dung are carefully reserved, as a manure for rice land; and the manure that is made from each kind of litter is kept in a separate dunghill. In the two months preceding, and in that following the winter solstice, the litter is dry grass, and the manure formed with it is called *Caradada Gobra*. Dry leaves of every kind of tree, except those that are prickly, and those of the *Govay* (*Goa*) or *Anacardium occidentale* Lin: are used as litter in the three following months, and form a manure which is called *Daryghena Gobra*. During the six remaining months, mostly of wet weather, the fresh leaves of trees are used for litter, and make a dung called *Hudi Gobra*, which is esteemed the best. The ashes of the family are kept in a separate pit, and are applied to different purposes. The cakes made of cow-dung are little used as fewel in this part of the country; but, to increase the quantity of manure, the women and boys follow the cattle while at pasture, and pick up the dung."

Buchanan had mentioned (February 24, 1801) that in this part of the country, the leaves of nelli or *Phyllanthus emblica* (present name *Emblica officinalis*) were used as manure in the areca-nut gardens where betel-leaf vines were also trained upon the areca palms.

During his stay at Sadashivagad (March 3, 1801), Buchanan collected the following information regarding preparation of manure in this part of Canara.

> **"Manure.** – In the rainy season the cattle are kept in the house, and, to increase the quantity of manure, are littered with fresh leaves. In the dry season they are shut up at night in pens, which are placed on the *Surd* lands, and are shifted once in four days. Every

morning some dry soil is mixed with the foregoing night's dung, and the whole is made smooth, that the cattle may lie clean. The manure collected in the rainy season is given to the soil of the first and second quality, which are always sown with rice after the dry-seed cultivation. The ashes of the family are kept separate, but are used for the same kind of land."

During his tour around Sirsi and Sonda, Buchanan mentioned (March 15, 1801) that the use of the leaves of nelli or *Phyllanthus emblica* tree as manure especially at the time of formation of new areca gardens was prevalent in this part of the *Haiga* country above the *Ghats*. Here, nelli leaves were also used to manure the cardamom plants (*Amomum repens*) that were planted between the areca palms in the areca-nut gardens.

While describing the state of agriculture in the more open (eastern) parts of the Sonda region, Buchanan gave the following description with regard to preparation of manure (March 16, 1801).

"Manure. – In the dry weather, the cattle are folded on the fields; in the rainy season they are taken within doors, and as a manure for the fields their dung is collected, and mixed with ashes, and the soil of the farmer's house. Those who have no gardens allow no litter: but the *Haiga Brahmans*, for the use of their gardens, litter the cattle at one season with fresh leaves, and at another with dry grass. The two manures thus formed are kept separate, and applied to different purposes. A want of attention to manure is a striking feature in the grain farmers of *Soonda*."

Buchanan entered the Mysore State on the 18th of March, 1801, as he crossed over from Canara to the Shimoga district and proceeded towards Nagara (Hyder Nagara, originally known as Bidderhally, and then as Bidderuru). Buchanan had noticed (March 25, 1801) that, likewise around Sirsi in Canara, nelli leaves were used as manure in this part of the Mysore State comprising Nagara, Sagara and Ikkeri. As regards various types of manure used in this part of the State, Buchanan wrote as follows (March 25, 1801):

> **"Treatment of the cattle and manure. March 25. –** The cattle are kept all the year in the house. In the rainy season, they are littered with green leaves. Fresh litter is every day added, but the stable is cleaned only once a week. This dung is collected in a pit, and is called *Sopina Gobra*, or leaf manure. During the two months preceding and the two following the winter solstice, the cattle are littered with hill grass, and cleaned once if four days. This dung also is collected in a separate pit, and is called *Hulu*, or *Soday Gobra*. In the hot and dry season the cattle are littered with dry leaves, and cleaned once in four days; the dung is generally spread upon the hollow roads leading into the villages, where it is trodden upon by man and beast, and is thereby much improved; but it renders the villages quite loathsome. This is called *Daraghina Gobra*. The grass (*Hulu*) dung is never used for rice land; but all the three are indiscriminately used for gardens."

With regard to preparation of manure around Shimoga, Buchanan gave the following description (April 2, 1801).

> **"Manure**. - The cattle are never littered; and the only manure used is their dung, collected in a pit, together with the grass and straw which they did not eat in the night. To these are added the ashes and sweepings of the farmer's house."

During his stay at Harihar (April 8-10, 1801), Buchanan ascertained the method of preparation of manure in the region and gave the following description.

> **"Cattle and manure**. – Many of the farmers keep no cows, but purchase all their cattle. They, of course, can sell at least one half of their straw to the *Brahmans* of the town, who in general keep many milch cows, and who in return sell the young oxen and the manure to the farmers. Although the cattle are always kept in the house, except during the two months immediately following the rains, no litter is used. Their dung is collected in pits, with the sweepings and ashes of the family, and sells for from six to twelve *Dudus* for

the load of a cart which is drawn by eight oxen, but which does not appear to contain more than a single-horse cart. The price is from about 5*d.* to half that amount. The farmers also hire flocks of sheep to manure their fields, and say, that for folding his flocks on a *Mar* of land, they give the shepherd one *Colaga* of *Jola;* this, however, must be a gross exaggeration."

With regard to preparation of manure around Hiriyur, Buchanan provided the following information (April 19, 1801).

"**Cattle and Manure**. - The village cattle during the whole year are kept in the house, but are not littered. Their dung is collected in pits, and mixed with the ashes and other soil of the family. This manure is reserved for the rice-land. The dry field gets nothing, except the dung of the sheep, which, at any season, are herded on it at night. A flock of 500 in two nights are supposed to manure fully a plough of land. The farmers say, that when they have not sheep of their own they hire in the flocks of the shepherds, and give them two or three *Fanams* for manuring the plough of land. But this is denied by the shepherds, who allege, that, except permission to feed their flocks on the fallow lands, they get nothing; and this, I believe, is true. The want of attention to increase the quantity of manure is a gross defect in the agriculture of *Heriuru*, and may account for the wretched produce of its field."

Buchanan had considered the practice of littering the cattle sheds with grasses, leaves, etc. as very beneficial to agriculture. While passing through Belur (May 13, 1801) in present Hassan district, he had commented upon the absence of this practice in the region as follows:

"**Cattle and manure.** – The only manure used here is from the dunghill, in which, with all the cow-dung, the ashes and sweepings of the house are collected. The cattle sleep the whole year in the house, but are never littered, which is a very great defect in the agriculture of a country.---"

From the above descriptions provided by Buchanan regarding the various types of manure used in the farmlands, it is apparent that in the drier districts it was mostly the leaves of the honge tree (*Pongamia pinnata*) in combination with a number of locally available shrubs and herbs that catered to the manure needs. This was understandable because in these districts with scanty rainfall, there were hardly any other tree species in the vicinity of the farmlands that were appropriate for this purpose, and as a result, various species of locally available shrubs and herbs including the hardy ones such as *Dodonaea viscosa* or *Calotropis gigantea* were utilized. With regard to the versatility of the honge tree to grow even in difficult sites, Buchanan had commented thus [Buchanan Vol. I, Page No. 8]: 'The only trees that grow spontaneously are the *Melia azadirachta*, and the *Robinia mitis*; the last of which flourishes both on the arid hills of *Carnatic*, and on the muddy banks of the *Ganges.*' In the districts falling in the high rainfall zone, there were, besides varieties of grass, sufficient numbers of tree species in and around the farmlands answering the requirement of manure. As a result, shrubs and herbs were not generally used for the purpose of manure in this region. Interestingly, leaves of the nelli tree (*Emblica officinalis*) were almost invariably used in the gardens of the high rainfall zone of both Canara and Mysore.

Buchanan also mentioned about another farmer-friendly tree occurring in the dry districts of the Mysore State, namely, the *Acacia nilotica* (karijali/babul).

Acacia nilotica/arabica (karijali/babul)

When travelling from Madras to Srirangapatna, Buchanan had passed through Mandya on 16th May, 1800. He had noticed the occurrence of the babul or karijali trees (then known as *Mimosa indica* of Lamarck) in the agricultural lands. Buchanan had commented as follows:

> "---This tree is allowed to grow promiscuously through the fields, and its branches are lopped off for fewel, and for repairing the fences. Its shade does not injure the crops, and its timber is valuable for making ploughs, and other instruments of agriculture."

While travelling from Srirangapatna to Periyapatna, Buchanan had come across (September 8, 1800) agricultural fields which were separated from each other either by hedges or by strips of land that had trees such as *Acacia nilotica*. He wrote as follows:

"-----. The custom here is to separate the fields either by hedges, or by leaving between them uncultivated spaces from four to ten feet wide, which are covered with *Mimosas*, or other trees; which adds greatly to the beauty of the country, and, by preserving the moisture, probably contributes to the fertility of the land. I think that I can every where observe traces either of the hedges, or of these woody spaces, except in a few spots covered with the *Elate sylvestris*, or wild date, and of these the soil is said to be saline.----."

Buchanan again came across agricultural lands interspersed with babul or karijali trees near Bannur (June 5, 1801) during his return journey to Madras.

"----. From thence to *Banuru* the level country widens, and is mostly arable; but little of it is watered. It looks very well, many of the fields being enclosed, and interspersed with *Babul* trees (*Mimosa indica* Lamarck). These do not injure the corn growing under them, and hinder so much ground only from being productive as is occupied by the diameter of their stems. Although it does not grow to a large size, the *Babul* is very useful in making the implements of agriculture. Its bark is valuable to the tanner. At reasonable distances, therefore, throughout the *Ragi* fields, young plants of it are allowed to grow."

TREES AS NURSE CROP

Among the various cash crops raised in Mysore and Canara, Betel-nut or Areca-nut was the most important. The best cultivable land with assured and sufficient water supply was chosen for this purpose. However, as the betel-nut palm is quite sensitive to intense sunlight, it was never planted directly in an open area but was introduced in a phased manner by creating an appropriate ambience with the help of trees providing lateral shade. During his journey, Buchanan had ascertained the methods of developing areca nut gardens in different parts of Mysore and Canara. Two of Buchanan's narrations, one from Mysore State and another from Canara, are described below.

During his stay at Chikkanayakanahalli (August 21, 1800), Buchanan had provided the following description of raising a betel-nut garden right from the nursery stage:

"**August 21. *Betel-nut*.** - The *Betel-nut* palm, or *Areca*, thrives best in the rich black mould called by the natives *Eray*, or *Krishna Bumi*. The natives here look upon it as a matter of indifference, whether or not, on digging a little depth, water may be found in the soil. All that is required, is to have a proper supply of water either from the reservoir, or by means of machinery.

"In the second month after the winter solstice, the nut intended for seed is cut; and, having been put in a heap, is for eight or ten days kept in the house. A seed-bed is then dug to the depth of a foot, and three inches of the mould is removed from the surface, which is then covered with a little dung. On this the nuts are placed with their eyes uppermost, and close to each other. They are then covered with an inch of mould, and for three months are watered every other day. The seedlings are then three or four inches high, and must be transplanted into a fresh bed that is prepared in the same manner; but in this they are placed a cubit distant from each other. Here they grow for three years, receiving water once every other day; and once a month they are cleaned from weeds, and have a little dung.

"One year after planting the seed, the ground that is intended for the garden must be dug to the depth of a cubit, and the soil exposed for two months. Young plantain trees (*Musa*) are then placed in it at 16 cubits distance from each other, and it is surrounded by a screen of coco-nut palms, and of Jack (*Artocarpus integrifolia*), lime, and orange trees, which are defended by a hedge of the *Euphorbium Tirucalli*, or milk-bush. At the same time seeds of the *Agashay*, or *Aeschynomene grandiflora*, are planted throughout the garden, at the distance of four cubits. When there is no rain, the garden must once in fifteen days be watered by channels made for the purpose. In the second month after the summer solstice of the third year, the young *Arecas* are fit for transplantation. Then throughout the garden, at the distance of 16 cubits, and in the middle between every two plantain trees, are formed pits, a cubit deep and a cubit wide. In each of these pits a young *Areca* is put, and it must be carefully raised from the seed-bed with much earth adhering to its roots; and, after it is placed, the pit must be filled with earth, and then receive a pot of water. The young *Arecas* are then between two and three feet high, and have four or five branches. If there be water in the reservoir, an irrigation once a month is sufficient; but the *Capily* must be used once in ten days, as the waterings given by it are but scanty. For three years afterwards the whole garden must be completely hoed twice annually. At the one hoeing, for every four *Arecas*, it must have a bullock-load of dung; and at the other hoeing, every tree must be allowed an ox-load of red soil. The mud of reservoirs is here thought to be very bad for the *betel-nut* garden. Ever afterwards the garden is hoed completely once a year only, and it is then manured with dung and red earth. At the intermediate period of six months, it is hoed near the trees, and has little dung. At the end of the first three years, the *Agashay* trees are cut. The plantains are always reserved; but, as the old stems are cut, which is always done in from 12 to 18 months, the young shoots are conducted to a distance from where the parent was originally placed; and when the garden is twenty years old, in these spots are planted other young *Arecas*, to supply the places of old ones when they decay. This second set are again supplanted by a third, growing where the first set did, and thus a constant succession is preserved. In a new garden, the *Areca* begins to bear fruit in nine years; but fourteen or fifteen years are required to bring forward those which are planted among old trees. They continue to bear for sixty or seventy years; but after having been twenty-five or thirty years in perfection, they begin to decay."

During his stay at Mangalore (January 22-29, 1801), Buchanan described the method of raising betel-nut plantation in the *Tulava* region as follows:

"**Cultivation of the *Areca* palm.** – Here the *Areca* or *Betel-nut* palm forms separate plantations, which are surrounded by some rows of the coco-nut tree, and is not scattered about the gardens, as in Malabar. The following is the manner of making one of these plantations, as described by the proprietors. Between the 17th of December, and the 13th of February, the seed must be collected from the trees that are at least fifty years old. Having been kept four days in the house, it is tied up in a *Moray*, or straw-bag, and is immersed for 25 days in the water of a well. In the mean time a small plot of rice ground is repeatedly ploughed until it be reduced to a fine mud, and is well manured with dung and ashes. In this mud the nuts are placed close to one another, with their eyes uppermost, and one half of them above the earth. Then the plot is covered with straw, and is watered once a day for a month. A piece of dry ground is then dug up with the hoe, and manured with dung and ashes. Into this the nuts, which have now sprouted, are transplanted at half a cubit's distance from each other. The nuts only are covered, and the sprouts are left projecting. For two months, if the soil be moist, it must be watered once in four days; if it be dry, once in three days is sufficient. Another piece of ground is in the mean time prepared; and at the end of the two months the young seedlings are removed thither, and placed at the distance of one cubit from each other. In this nursery they remain eight months; and once in four days, when there is no rain, they are watered. In the mean while the garden is prepared by inclosing it with a dry hedge of prickly bushes. Within the hedge a row of coco-nut palms is planted, each being 24 cubits from the other. Within these, at 10 cubits distance from each other, are formed pits, two cubits in diameter, and two cubits deep. In the bottom of each of these is put a young *Areca*; all its roots are covered with fine mould, and it is manured with a little dung. This is between the 19th of October and the 16th of November, at the close of the rainy season. Every fourth day the pits must be watered, while the sun is excluded by branches and leaves. At the end of six months some dung must be given, and the weeds removed by the hand. Whenever there is no rain the waterings are to be continued; and twice a year the trees must be manured, and the weeds ought to be removed from near their roots. In two years the pits are filled up with the manure. At the end of five years another set of pits is made, one between every two of the old ones; and in these is placed another set of young plants, and managed as the first set. At this second planting some plantain trees (*Musas*) are set in the garden, but not above forty for the hundred *Arecas*. Near the hedge, in a line with the coco-nut palms, are also put some *Jack* (*Artocarpus integrifolia*) and *Mango* (*Mangifera indica*) trees. When ten years old, the *Areca* begins to produce fruit; but until the fifteenth year does not arrive at perfection. For thirty-five years it continues in full bearing. From its 50th year until its death, which happens in from its 70th to its 100th year, the quantity of fruit gradually diminishes, but its quality rather improves. The trees in full fruit produce annually three bunches, which ripen in succession between the 19th of October and the 16th of December. Each bunch contains from 30 to 100 nuts; so that, according to the natives, 200 nuts may be taken as the average produce of an *Areca* when it is in vigour. When the *Mango* and *Jack* trees have grown up, the pepper vines are usually put round them. Some people plant them also against the *Areca*, but they diminish its produce. *Yams* (*Dioscoreas*) are planted near the hedge."

TREES AS SUPPORT TO CLIMBERS

Betel-leaf vine

During his stay at Srirangapatna between 20th May and 5th June, 1800, Buchanan had ascertained the method of developing a betel-leaf garden.

He gave a detailed description of the process including that of planting trees which eventually serve as the support for the betel-leaf vines to climb up.

"**Betel-leaf gardens.** – Near *Seringapatam* the *Betel-leaf* gardens (*Piper betel*) are not numerous. They are invariably formed on rice ground; and a *Cabbay* soil, or a mixture of *Cabbay* with *Marulu*, best answers the purpose. The *Betel-leaf-vine* is sometimes planted against the *Betel-nut-palm*, in which case it pays no rent; but when it is planted by itself, a rent is fixed by an agreement between the officers of revenue and the cultivator. In this case, the garden is surrounded by a hedge of the *Euphorbium Tirucalli*; and a well is dug, from whence the garden is watered by pots. In *Chaitra*, from the 26th of March till the 23rd of April, the garden throughout is dug one cubit deep, and the grass and roots are carefully removed. Having allowed it to rest for a month and having obtained a shower of rain, hoe it with the *Yella Kudali*, and make it smooth. Holes, one cubit and a half in diameter, and three inches deep, are then formed throughout the field, at the distance of five cubits. In each of these is laid down a bundle of five cuttings of the *Betel-leaf-vine*, a cubit and a half in length, and tied slightly together in the middle. A thin covering of earth is then put on the middle of each bundle, both ends of the cuttings being left bare. After this, for one month, the holes must be shaded from the sun, by covering them with leaves and branches, and each hole must daily receive two pots of water. Near each row of holes, a drill must be made with the *Yella Kudali*; and in this must be planted, at every half cubit's distance, the seeds of the *Agashay* (*Aeschynomene grandiflora*), *Harwana* (*Erythrina indica*, Lamarck), *Bura* and *Nugay* (*Guilandiana Moringa*), which must be slightly covered. This whole process must be finished in *Vaisakha*, which this year ends with the 23rd of May. Each of the holes must everyday receive half a pot of water, except when it rains; and on the 15th day must have as much cow-dung and ashes mixed as the cultivator can lift between his two hands joined. After this manuring, when there is no rain, the garden must once every other day be watered. The manuring must be repeated once a month till the shoots are six months old; at the same time the garden must be weeded, and the earth in the holes loosened with a sharp stick. In each hole, at the end of six months from planting, must be put two sticks, three cubits high, on which the young vines may climb. At the end of the year, these sticks are pulled out; the vines are then put upon the young trees; and every month, as they grow, must be tied up to the stems. Once a year, two cubits of the part of the vine that is nearest the ground must be laid down, and buried in the earth. The plant begins to produce ripe leaves in the twenty-fifth month, and continues productive at all seasons, and for many years. One of the men present, who is about fifty years of age, possessed a garden that had been planted by his father when a young man."

In the betel-leaf gardens around Kolar, which Buchanan had visited during the period from 8th to 11th July, 1800, the betel-leaf vines were trained upon the trees of *Agashay*, or *Aeschynomene grandiflora* (present name, *Sesbania grandiflora*); *Nugay*, or *Guilandiana Moringa* (present name, *Moringa oleifera*); and *Varjepu*, or *Erythrina indica*, E. M. Here also, these supporting trees were raised from seed sown adjacent to where the cuttings of the Betel-leaf-vine were planted in a manner almost similar to the method adopted in the betel-leaf gardens around Srirangapatna, as narrated in the preceding paragraph.

During his stay at Periyapatna (September 11-13, 1800), Buchanan had observed that betel-leaf vines and areca palms were grown in the same plot. However, the betel-leaf-vines were introduced only after the areca palms were fifteen years old. Areca palm begins to decay at an age of about forty-five years, but at that time the betel-leaf vine remains quite vigorous. Hence, the decaying areca palm is removed carefully to ensure that the vine is not injured. Near the place of the palm that has been removed is made a small hole, in which either a young areca seedling is planted or two areca nuts are placed as seed for germination. In order to support the vine, during the fifteen years which are required to bring forward the new palm, a large branch of the *Haruana* or the *Erythrina*, is stuck in the ground, and watered for two three days; when it strikes root, the *Erythrina* branch serves the purpose of support for the vine.

Pepper vine

During his camp at Mangalore (January 22-29, 1801), Buchanan ascertained the method of raising pepper vines and described it as follows:

> **"Black-pepper.** – The pepper is managed as follows. Between the 24th of May and the 22nd of June, the ground near the tree upon which it is to be trained is dug with a hoe. Then two, three, or four cuttings of the pepper vine, each a cubit long, are put in the ground, one end of them being allowed to project. They are then covered with grass. This is done when the rainy season commences. A month afterwards they get a little dung. As the vines shoot, they are tied to the tree. When the dry season commences, they must be watered every second day, until a year old, after which they require water once in four days. Twice a year also they must get manure of dung and leaves; and long grass, or bushes, must be prevented from growing near their roots; but there is no occasion to dig or plough the whole ground. They begin to bear in the fifth year; but are not in full crop until the eighth. If the worms attack the vine, they die in twelve or fifteen years; but otherwise they live twenty-five, and all the while produce good crops. When any vine dies, a new one is planted in its stead. Here they are trained upon the *Pongary* or *Hongary* (*Erythrina*), the *Nuriga* (*Moringa*), *Jack* (*Artocarpus*), *Mango* (*Mangifera*), *Areca*, coco-nut, and tamarind. The first is, however, most commonly employed, and in this country lives for fifty years. It is not customary here to prune the trees upon which the pepper is trained.---"

While travelling in the *Haiga* country in the northern part of Canara, Buchanan had come across pepper vines being managed in the forest areas. These were wet evergreen forests that naturally harbored the black pepper vines. The neighboring villagers, by resorting to thinning of the forest and manipulation of the canopy, had developed the technique of training these vines upon some selected forest trees. Buchanan had given the description of such a pepper plantation near *Mirzee* (Mirjan) situated between Kumta and Hiregutti (February 25, 1801).

"**Pepper growing spontaneously.**-The pepper-plant (*Piper nigrum*) seems to grow spontaneously on the sides of all the narrow vallies in the interior of *Haiga*, where the soil is so rich and moist to produce lofty trees close to each other, by which a constant coolness is retained. In such places the pepper-vine runs along the ground and the roots of bushes, and propagates itself entirely by striking its roots into the soil, and then again sending out new shoots. The natives say, that without assistance it cannot ascend a tree; and that, unless it is exposed in such a situation to sun and air, it never produces flowers. In order to procure fruit from a hill which spontaneously produces the pepper-vine, the proprietor cuts all the underwood and bushes, and leaves only the large trees, and a number of the young ones sufficient to exclude the violence of sun, but to allow free circulation of air. Four cubits from tree to tree is reckoned a proper distance. The ends of the vines, which were lying on the ground, are then tied up to the nearest trees. Any kind of tree answers the purpose; but those of eight inches or a foot in diameter are preferred, as it is easy to climb such for the purpose of gathering the pepper. A quantity of leaves are then placed round the root of the vine, to rot, and to serve as manure. In the course of the year the vine, so far it has been tied, strikes its roots into the bark of the tree; but the shoots above that, hang down. Twice a year afterwards, these are tied up, and strike root, till they spread over all the large branches of the tree. In places where no vines have naturally sprung, the owner, after having dug a small spot round the tree to loosen the earth, propagates them by planting slips near the roots of the trees on which he wishes them to climb. The early part of the rainy season is the time proper for this operation. In five years, after having been managed in this manner, a hill begins to produce fruit, and in eight years is in full bearing. The vines live about thirty years; when others, that are found creeping on the ground in their natural state, are tied up in their stead; or, where these happen to be wanting, shoots or cuttings are planted near the trees. There is no difference in the quality between the pepper springing spontaneously from the seed, and that growing from cuttings; nor is the pepper growing in gardens either better or worse than that growing on a hill, managed as I am describing. These hills producing pepper require no trouble, but the tying up of the plants, keeping the forest clear of underwood, and collecting the pepper. --"

TREES AND OTHER PLANTS FOR FENCING

During his journey, Buchanan had made it a point to observe the state of protection of agricultural land by means of trees or other plants which formed a vegetative barricade or live-hedge. He had underscored the importance of such a hedge or fence not only for physically protecting the farmland but also as a measure of moisture conservation. Before entering the Mysore State, as he was passing through dry agricultural lands near the hilly terrain of Venkatagiri in the present state of Andhra Pradesh, he had made the following observations (May 4, 1800).

> "-----These lands appear, however, to be perfectly fitted for the English manner of cultivation; and in order to preserve some moisture in the ground, they ought to be enclosed with hedges, and planted with hedge-rows. The *Euphorbium Tirucalli*, common in the country, makes a beautiful fence; and I think it probable, that the mahogany and the chestnut would be found to answer in hedge-rows, as they are both natives of hilly countries, and warm climates."

After entering the Mysore State, as he was proceeding towards *Tayculum* (present Tekal, in Kolar district), Buchanan made the following observations regarding the usefulness of forming hedges around farmlands with *Tirucalli* and Aloes (May 6, 1800).

> "**Hedges of the *Tirucalli*. Aloes.** – The *Euphorbium Tirucalli*, with very little trouble, makes excellent fences. In the beginning of the rainy season, cuttings are planted in a trench, which is dug where the fence is intended to grow, and they take root without

any further trouble. No cattle will eat this plant; so that it is easily preserved, and in one year becomes a tolerable fence. The natives here plant also many aloes (*agave vivipara*) in their hedges, and use their leaves for making cordage. It forms a strong defence against both man and beast, and thrives better in the arid soil of *Mysore*, than in any other place that I have seen; its *Canarese*, or *Karnataca* name is *Ravana Meshid.*"

Buchanan also mentioned (May 7, 1800) about houses in Malur surrounded by strong hedges fortified with spiny climbers such as *Caesalpinia lacerans* Roxb. MSS (present name, *Pterolobium hexapetalum* - Baadubakka) and *Mimosa saponaria* (present name, *Acacia concinna* – Seegekai).

When travelling through Maddur (May 15, 1800), Buchanan had noticed poorly maintained and ineffective fences separating agricultural lands belonging to different owners.

"----Many of the fields are surrounded by hedges; but these are not kept in such repair as to be fences against cattle. Perhaps they are meant merely to distinguish the fields of different proprietors, or tenants, and to contain the *Agave vivipara*, and *Jatropha curcas*, that are wanted for the use of the country, and of which they chiefly consist."

Buchanan had noticed similar poorly maintained fences in and around Mandya that he was travelling through on the next day (May 16, 1800).

"The hedges here, like those I saw yesterday, are very bad fences, and are made of *Euphorbium antiquorum*. When the ground is sown, the farmers fill up the gaps with thorns cut from the *Mimosa indica* of Lamarck.---"

During his stay at Srirangapatna between 20th May and 5th June, 1800, Buchanan had come across a betel-leaf garden surrounded by a hedge of *Euphorbium tirucalli.*

During his stay in Channapatna (June 11, 1800), Buchanan had ascertained that the betel-nut gardens are fenced with a hedge of *Euphorbium tirucalli* or *Jatropha curcas*.

During his stay at Kolar (July 8-11, 1800), Buchanan had observed that the betel-leaf gardens were enclosed by a hedge of the *Euphorbium tirucalli*, and of the *Arundo tibialis* (Roxb: MSS.) (present name, *Phragmites karka* – Hulugila hullu/Nal)

As already mentioned in a preceding paragraph, during his stay at Chikkanayakanahalli, Buchanan had observed that the betel-nut gardens were surrounded by a screen of coco-nut palms, and of Jack (*Artocarpus integrifolia*), lime, and orange trees, which were defended by a hedge of the *Euphorbium Tirucalli*, or milk-bush.

During his stay at Periyapatna (September 11-13, 1800), Buchanan had observed that the betel-nut gardens were surrounded with a hedge of *Euphorbium tirucalli*, and some rows of young coco-nut palms.

As Buchanan was travelling from HD Kote towards Nanjangud, and was passing through the neighbourhood of Hampapura (September 20, 1800), he had seen partially abandoned agricultural lands which once had very good fences. He described the general state of the fences in this part of the State as follows:

"**Fences.** – All the high grounds that I have seen south from the *Cavery*, as well as those in many places north from the river, have evidently been once fenced with quickest hedges. Some of these at this place are very fine; and the natives, being sensible of the advantage of the shelter in preserving a moisture in their fields, have allowed the *Tirucalli* to grow twenty feet high. When from its height it has become too open at the roots, they plant in the openings the *Euphorbium antiquorum*, which grows well under the shade of the other; and both united make a good and very beautiful fence. The hedges of the country in general, even where they are kept up as fences, are in a very slovenly condition, and are ruined by being overgrown with the *Convolvulus*, and other rank climbing plants."

When travelling through Belur (in present Hassan district) on May 13, 1801, Buchanan learned about the practice of rearing the Cochineal insect in some parts of the State. His observations on the practice which had adverse impact on the hedges of agricultural lands are reproduced below.

"**Cochineal.** – I found here two men whom an officer now stationed at *Arcot* employed in rearing cochineal. They have been in this country one year, have sent to their employer fifteen *Maunds*, have fifteen *Maunds* ready for sale, and, before the insects have consumed all the *Nopals* (*Cactus*) that are near the town, they expect to have ten *Maunds* more. When this happens, they will carry two men's load of branches filled with the insect, and apply these to the *Nopals* of some other place; where they will remain until the insects breed, and consume all the plants. The *Nopals* have been raised by the farmers as fences round their gardens, but were sold by the officers of revenue for four *Bahadury Pagodas*, or about a guinea and a half. So soon all the plants have been consumed, such of the insects as have not been collected will perish; and the *Amildar* says, that he will then compel the farmers to plant new hedges of the *Nopal*; but I suspect that few plants will be reared, unless the farmers get a large share of the profits, as indeed they ought in reason to do. The hedges will grow up in three years, when it is expected that some other person rearing the insect will come and buy the plants.

"This seems to me to be the most rational plan of any that has been hitherto proposed for rearing the cochineal in India; and to be deserving of the attention and encouragement of government. The men employed here say, that the young insects ought to be put upon the new hedges immediately after the rainy season is past. In six months they will have increased so, that they may begin to be collected; and a year more will elapse before the whole plants are consumed. During the course of this year, whenever a leaf is fully loaded, it ought to be cut, and the insects scraped from it with a small stick, and collected in a basket. While they are in this, a little boiling water is poured on them, by which they are killed. They are then well agitated in the basket, to remove the hair with which they are covered, and dried for two days in the sun, when they are fit for sale. These men say, that, all expenses included, the cochineal, thus prepared, will cost here three *Madras Pagodas* a *Maund* of forty *Seers*, each weighing twenty-four *Rupees*, which is rather less than 11*d.* a pound. The cochineal is of the bad kind that has lately been introduced into India, and the plant is the *Cactus* that is the aboriginal of the country."

The above observations of Buchanan are significant; while he was in favour of encouraging the practice of rearing cochineal, he was critical of the arrangement by which the entire income was appropriated by the government without giving any share of it to the farmers who grew and nurtured the *Cacti* (Nopals) around their farmlands. In order to ensure sustained interest of the farmers in growing and maintaining the *Cacti* in their hedges, the government ought to have shared a portion of the income with the farmers. Absence of such a policy must have affected the quality of the hedges, which deteriorated year after year. [**Note:** A crimson-red compound known as Carmine derived from the Cochineal insect is used in the cosmetic industry for making lipstick.]

Chapter 7

ORCHARDS, GARDENS AND AVENUE TREES

Buchanan had entered the Mysore State on 5th May, 1800. As he travelled through Bethamangala (*Baydamungulum*) and Tekal (*Tayculum*), he had found the appearance of the country rather barren with extensive rocky hills and covered at places with low level scrub comprising *Albizia amara* ['copse wood, chiefly of the *Mimosa* which I call *Tuggulu*]. The arable lands were mostly dry lands. Water was scarce, and the limited watered land was occupied by *betel-leaf* gardens, and some sugar-cane. On seeing some healthy trees in the farmlands, Buchanan had recognized the immense capability of the soil. He had commented near *Tayculum:* or Tekal (May 6, 1800) as follows:

> "The nakedness of the country does not proceed from any incapacity in the soil to produce trees; for to-day I observed many that were really fine. The *Tamarind, Mango, Pipal*, and *Robinia mitis* thrive well."

Buchanan was quite impressed with the way the villagers took care of the mango and other fruit trees grown in their premises. He made the following comments as he passed through Kadugodi (*Catcolli*) on 9th May, 1800.

"----The hedges surrounding the villages, in this part of the country, rise very high and thick, so as almost entirely to conceal the mud walls, which enlivens the prospect considerably, especially as at the villages there are a good many *mango* trees. The planting of these, or other fruit trees, is here attended with a considerable expense; as every young tree is surrounded by a mud wall, three or four feet high, and perhaps twenty in diameter; and in the dry season the plant requires to be watered, every second or third day, for three years."

After reaching Bangalore on 10th May, 1800, Buchanan visited the gardens developed by Haider Ali and Tippu Sultan the next day. Buchanan did not mention the name of the gardens as the Lalbagh gardens, as they are known nowadays.

"**Gardens. 11th May.** – I visited the gardens made by the late Mussulman princes, *Hyder* and *Tippoo*. They are extensive, and divided into square plots separated by walks, the sides of which are ornamented with fine cypress trees. The plots are filled with fruit trees, and pot-herbs. The Mussulman fashion is to have a separate piece of ground allotted for each kind of plant. Thus one plot is entirely filled with rose trees, another with pomegranates, and so forth. The walks are not graveled, and the cultivation of the whole is rather slovenly; but the people say, that formerly the gardens were well kept. Want of water is the principal defect of these gardens; for in this arid country every thing, during the dry season, must be artificially watered. The garden of *Tippoo* is supplied from three wells, the water of which is raised by the *Capily*, or leather-bag, fastened to a cord passing over a pulley, and wrought by a pair of bullocks, which descend an inclined plane. This, the workmen say, is a much more effectual machine than the *Yatam*. *Hyder's* garden is watered from a reservoir, without the assistance of machinery. The taste of *Hyder* accorded more with the English, than that of his son. His walks are wider, his cypress trees are not so much crowded; and in the means for watering the plots there is not so much masonry, or bricklayer's work, employed. There is, indeed, so much of these in the parts of *Tippoo's* garden which he probably considered the finest, as almost to cover the ground, and to leave nothing but holes, as it were, through which the trees grow.

"Fruits. -In this climate the cypress and the vine grow luxuriantly, and the apple and peach both produce fruit; the former much better, and the latter much worse than at *Calcutta*. Some pine and oak plants, lately introduced from the Cape of Good Hope, seem to be thriving. I think there can be little doubt, but that in this country all the valuable plants of the *Levant* would succeed. The people at the gardens could form no estimate of the quantity of grapes produced by any number of vines."

It is interesting to note that Buchanan had found the climate of Bangalore similar to that of the Levant, known for its Mediterranean climate that is conducive to growth of trees, especially varieties of fruit trees. Buchanan's account reveals that Bangalore and its surroundings did not have much greenery in the beginning of the nineteenth century. However, having seen the trees in the gardens raised by Haider Ali and Tipu Sultan and considering the relatively cooler climate of Bangalore, Buchanan had made an assessment about Bangalore's potential to harbor trees which eventually proved to be correct, as during the next two hundred years Bangalore gradually transformed into a green city, having earned the title of 'Garden City of India'.

[**Note:** Levant is the Eastern Mediterranean region of Western Asia.]

As Buchanan proceeded further from Bangalore towards Srirangapatna, and passed by Bidadi (*Wiridy* or *Biridy*) on 13th May, he travelled through a valley that 'consists of fields, swelling like the grounds in Kent, and contains many scattered trees, *mangoes* (*mangifera*), *banyans* (*Ficus bengalensis*), and the like.' On 15th May, Buchanan saw pretty extensive plantations of palm (coco-nut) and fruit trees near Maddur (*Mudur*). He also came across a flower garden which he described as follows:

"Flower gardens. – Although the *Nerium odorum* is very common by the sides of rivers in most parts of the *Mysore* dominions, I found a garden here, of about an acre in extent, which was planted with nothing else. The flowers are dedicated to the temple, and a garland-maker is paid by a merchant to gather them for the use of the god. This is one of the deeds called charity by the *Hindus*. This plant has usually been taken for the *oleander*, which, I believe, is not a native of India.'

During his stay at Srirangapatna (May 17 to June 5, 1800), Buchanan had ascertained about various aspects of agriculture in the neighbouring areas. As regards, fruit growing trees or orchards, he had collected the following information.

"**Orchards.** – In the *Tayngana Tota*, or orchards, are cultivated the following articles:

Canarese names.	Botanical names.	*Synonyma.*
Tayngana	*Cocos Nucifera*	*Coco-nut.*
Adicai	*Areca Catechu*	*Betel-nut, Supari* of the *Mussulmans.*
Balay	*Musa*	Plantain tree.
Nimbay	*Citrus*	Lime.
Kictalay	*Citrus*	Sweet orange.
Hayralay	*Citrus*	Bitter orange.
Jambu	*Psidium*	*Guava.*
Dalimbay	*Punica Granatum*	Pomegranate.
Hulusu	*Artocarpus integrifolia*	*Jack.*
Mau	*Mangifera*	Mango.
Nerulu	*Calyptranthes Cariophyllifolia* W.	
Nelli	*Phyllanthus Emblica*	

Hunishay	Tamarindus	Tamarind.
Amuttay. Humtica	Spondias dulcis.	

[**Note:** Buchanan had used the words *Tayngana Tota* to mean orchards perhaps because coco-nut trees were ubiquitous in all fruit gardens of that time.]

"In the *Ashta gram Talucs,* no fruit gardens of any consequence are remaining; these having all perished during the late wars. The soil favourable for them is low ground in narrow valleys, where water can easily be procured by digging a few feet. If this ground cannot be had, rice lands may be converted into orchards. In the neighbourhood of *Seringapatam,* however, there is much ground fit for gardens, where, by digging from one to four cubits, water can always be obtained. The soil must be *Eray,* or rich black clay. In making these gardens, it has been customary for the government to advance money to the farmer. The young trees are planted in rows; and between these are set plantain trees, with the produce of which, at the end of the year, the farmer pays back the advance. The *Coco* and *Betel-nut* palms are called *Vara,* and pay to government one half of the produce. The plantain pays three *Sultana Fanams* (2*s*. 0.177*d*.) for the hundred trees. The fruits of the mango, orange, &c. belong entirely to the farmer; but it is said, that the *Amildars* expect to be supplied for their own use, although they do not bring anything to accompt for these trees."

Regarding flower gardens in the neighbourhood of Srirangapatna, Buchanan gave the following account.

"**Flower gardens**. – The *Huvina,* or flower gardens, are cultivated near towns and populous places which afford a market for their produce. In other situations, small spots are planted with flowers for the use of the temples. It is only where the flowers are sold, that any rent is exacted for the soil. High grounds, that can be watered with pots from a well, are chosen for flower gardens, and the red soil is reckoned the most favourable."

While describing the method of raising betel-nut garden near Channapatna (June 11, 1800), Buchanan pointed out the role fruit-growing trees in improving the soil of the garden.

> "These plantations are interspersed with coco-nut, mango, lime, jack, and *Humteca* (*Spondias dulcis*) trees, which add to the shade, and to the freshness of the soil."

While describing the method of raising coco-nut plantations in the neighbourhood of Channapatna (June 11, 1800), Buchanan had mentioned that a number of vegetables and agricultural crops were also grown beneath these plantations. He further added that 'Mango and jack trees are also planted in these gardens, but greatly to their prejudice; for no cultivation can be carried on under these trees'.

During his return journey to Madras, Buchanan had passed through Malavalli where he visited the royal orchards on 8th June, 1801. He described as follows:

> "**Orchards of the late *Sultans*.** – *Hyder* gave *Malawully* in *Jaghire* to his son *Tippoo*, and of course it enjoyed considerable favour, and contained a thousand houses. Adjoining to the town is a very fine reservoir, that gives a constant supply of water to a fruit-garden which the *Sultan* planted. This is of great extent; but the soil is poor; and some of it is indeed so bad, that the trees have died, and the ground has been again converted into rice-fields. The establishment kept in this garden consists of one *Daroga*, or superintendant; one writer; and ten labourers, who, as they cultivate the rice-fields, are not able to keep the fruit trees in decent order, much less to prevent the walks from being in a most slovenly condition. The trees are 2400 in number; and of these one half are *Mangoes*. They are loaded with fruit, and some of the oranges are very fine. The *Mangoes* that I saw were but ordinary. One kind, if the account of the superintendant is to be credited, is very curious. It annually produces two crops, one in the hot season, the other during the rains. In the centre of the garden is a small, but neat cottage (*Bungalo*), from which grass walks diverge in all directions."

ARECA-NUT, COCO-NUT AND MANGO PLANTATIONS

Areca-nut and coco-nut constituted the principal horticultural crops of both Mysore State and Canara. Mango was also an important crop, perhaps next to areca-nut and coco-nut. Areca-nut requires very good soil with assured availability of water. In the maidan areas of the Mysore State, it was grown in level areas with easy access to underground water or near water reservoirs. The principal areca-nut growing areas in this region were Channapatna, Madhugiri, Chikkanayakanahalli, Periyapatna, Halthore (in present Hassan district). In the Ghat areas of the State, such as in Nagara, Sagara, Hodalla (near Thirthahalli), etc., areca-nut cultivation was very common in the vallies which had perennial sources of water. In Canara, areca nut was planted almost throughout, both below and above the *Ghats*, in the vallies where water supply was generally assured. Certain hill areas with assured water supply in the dry season were also planted with areca-nut. In both Mysore State and Canara, betel-leaf was also planted in some areca-nut plantations but this practice was not very common. In Colar district, although areca-nut plantations were not common, betel-leaf gardens were raised in areas with good water supply. It has already been mentioned in the preceding chapter (*Chapter 6*) that development of areca-nut plantation was done with a lot of care and planning in a phased manner to ensure that the areca nut plants are not adversely affected by direct sun light.

As regards Coco-nut plantations, as already mentioned in the previous chapter, a few lines of coco-nut trees were usually planted surrounding the areca-nut plantations. In addition, coco-nut plantations (palm) were also raised in areas with relatively good soil with sufficient moisture. Sandy soil was considered better for coco-nut plantations. Important coco-nut growing areas in the Mysore State were Channapatna and Chikkanayakanahalli; Sira and Kankanahalli (Kanakapura) also had some coco-nut gardens. In Canara, the coastal sandy areas and river-sides below the *Ghats* were ideal for coco-nut plantations.

In his travel-diaries Buchanan had mentioned about having seen mango trees in a number of places. It was quite commonly planted in orchards, on the periphery of areca-nut plantations, and also in homesteads. During his journey towards Doddaballapur that started from Bangalore on 3rd July,

1800, Buchanan's first halt was in a village called *Agara*, where 'a great many mangoes are raised for the Bangalore market.' Buchanan also mentioned about a fine mango grove surrounding a tank (*Colam*) situated half a mile away from the town *Caluru* (probably Kaiwara) in present Chikkaballapur district.

In a query raised by Buchanan regarding the number of trees contained in the gardens, Mr. Ravenshaw, the collector of the southern division of Canara, had furnished the following figures in respect of the southern division as per the survey done during 1792-93: Coco-nut – 695,060, Areca-nut – 1,155,850, Mango – 59,772, Sundries – 54, 362, and Pepper vines - 368,828. Mr. Ravenshaw had also added that since the last survey of 1792-93 the number of trees, in each description, was at least double of what was mentioned above.

AVENUE TREES

During his travel through Mysore, Buchanan had on one occasion come across avenue trees. He saw an avenue of mango and tamarind trees beside a road between *Caluru* (near Kolar) and a *Colam* (water tank) situated half a mile away from the town. Buchanan had also mentioned about the existence of avenue trees that had earlier sheltered the road between Melkote and Tonnur. Stumps of these trees were still visible during his visit to Tonnur from Melkote (August 31, 1800). Since Buchanan's travel was mostly along the important roads of the Mysore State, the fact that a keen observer like him had not noticed much of avenue trees during his long journey indicates that avenue planting was not very common in the State during that time.

In Canara, Buchanan had come across avenue trees on two occasions. While describing the appearance of the country near Udupi (February 11, 1801), Buchanan wrote as follows: "----The roads are execrable; but, like many of those in *Canara*, are shaded by fine rows of trees, especially of the *Vateria indica*; which, being now in full blossom, makes the most beautiful avenues that I have ever seen.---"

While travelling from Udupi to Brahmavara (February 12, 1801), Buchanan once again came across avenue trees which he described as follows: "----I soon came to gently rising hills, free of woods; but the road was finely sheltered by avenues of the beautiful *Vateria indica*, called here *Dupada Maram*, or the resin tree.---"

[**Note:** Excellent avenue plantations of **Vateria indica** (saldhupa), similar to the ones in Canara as described by Buchanan, had also adorned some of the roads of Sagar, Soraba, Hosanagara and Thirthahalli of the Mysore State. These plantations were reportedly raised during the reign of the Keladi Nayakas (1499-1763), who incidentally had ruled the coastal regions also. The two avenue plantations that Buchanan had seen near Udupi were probably raised during their rule. Apparently the route that Buchanan had taken in the Nagara region of the Mysore State did not harbor any of those avenue trees, or such trees had completed their life by the time of Buchanan's visit of the region.]

Chapter 8

TREES SUPPORTING ECONOMIC ACTIVITIES

During his journey through Mysore and Canara, in addition to learning in detail about various crops grown and farming practices prevalent in different regions, Buchanan had also given special emphasis on learning about the other economic activities that were pursued by the inhabitants. Some of these activities such as processing of agro-produce were by and large performed by the farmers themselves; but many others were performed by people as their primary profession. Some activities came under the exclusive domain of certain communities. The important economic activities of that period as noted by Buchanan were smelting of iron ore, manufacture of steel, textile industry (dyeing and printing), leather works (tanning), distillation of spirituous liquor, processing of agricultural produce, etc. Buchanan's writings reveal that the primary source of energy for carrying out these activities was firewood or charcoal derived from various trees and other plants. Buchanan had also noticed that while some activities required forest products such as dyes, *Lac*, tannins, etc., some others required certain parts of trees or plants as secondary inputs in order to facilitate or accelerate the activities. Based on his observations and interactions with knowledgeable people, Buchanan mentioned about these plant products in minute detail.

SMELTING OF IRON ORE

Smelting of iron ore was an important activity during the times of Haider Ali and Tipu Sultan, as iron was used in considerable quantities for the manufacture of armaments; there was also increasing demand for varieties of tools including agricultural implements made from iron. There were two sources of the iron ore; during the rainy season, ore particles commonly known as 'black sand' used to deposit in the stream beds from which it was collected and taken to the nearby site where the furnace (forge) was set up. It was also procured from the original ore body that normally occurred along the reefs of hillocks. In order to minimize the cost of transportation of the ore, the furnace for smelting was usually set up as near the source of the ore as possible, provided adequate tree growth for preparing charcoal was available in the vicinity. In this regard, Buchanan had commented near Bethamangala after entering the Mysore State (May 5, 1800): 'I am informed, that in every part of the country the black sand ore of iron is brought down by the torrents; but that it is smelted in such places only as abound with woods.'

During his journey through Mysore and Canara, Dr. Francis Buchanan had given detailed account of mining as well as smelting of iron ore that was carried out in various places of Mysore State. From Buchanan's account, the intensity of mining and smelting appeared to have been relatively high in the areas which now fall in Magadi of Ramanagara district, and in Tumkur and Chitradurga districts, although there were activities in other places also such as near Shimoga (Chandragutti), Ramanagara (Channapatna, Ramanagara) and Mysore (*Culia Betta*, *Mota Betta* and *Hiten Betta*, situated in the vicinity of Hampapura). Francis Buchanan provided the following information regarding the mining and smelting of iron in areas around Magadi that he had visited (June 13, 1800).

> **"Iron mines**. - On my way I examined some iron forges, of which there are many in the hilly tract of country; and from a man, who employs twelve labourers, I procured the following account of the operations performed on the ore. The iron is made partly from the black sand which is found in the rainy season in the channels of all the torrents in the country; and partly from an ore which is found

at *Ghettipura*, two cosses from *Magadi*. During the four months of heavy rains, four men were able to collect as much sand as a furnace can smelt in the remainder of the year. In order to separate the earth and sand, which are always mixed with it in the channel of the torrent, it requires to be washed. These men get ten *Fanams* or *6s. 8½d.* a month, and the nature of their service is similar to that of the farmer's servants, being bound by occasional advances of money to continue in the employment of the master. During the remaining eight months of the year, they work at the forge."

With regard to mining activities in and around the present Tumkur district, Buchanan wrote (August 13, 1800) as follows:

"**Iron mines**. - Iron is smelted in various places of the following *Talucs*, or districts; *Madhu-giri*, *Chin'-narayan'-durga*, *Hagalawadi*, and *Devaraya-durga*. In the first two districts the iron is chiefly made from the black-sand which the small torrents formed in the rainy season bring down from the rocks. In the two latter districts, it is made from an ore called here *Cany Callu*, which is found on the hill *Kindalay Guda*, near *Muga-Nayakana-Cotay* in the *Hagalawadi* district. A little of the same iron ore is also procured from a hill, called *Kaymutty*, near *Muso-conda* in the district *Chica-nayakana-Hully*.

"The manner of smelting the iron-ore, and rendering it fit for the use of blacksmith, is the same here as near *Magadi*. The people belonging to the smelting-house are four bellows-men, three men who make charcoal, and three women and one man who collect and wash the sand. They work only during the four months in which the sand is to be found; and for the remainder of the year they cultivate the ground, or supply the inhabitants of towns with fire-wood. The four men relieve each other at the bellows; but the most skilful person takes out the iron and builds up the furnace; on which account his allowance is greater. In each furnace the workman puts first a basket (about half a bushel) of charcoal. He then takes up as much of the black sand as he can lift with both his hands joined, and puts in double that quantity. He next puts in another basket of charcoal, and the fire is urged with the bellows. When the first charcoal that has been given burns down, he puts in the same quantity of sand, and one basket of charcoal; and does this again, so soon as the furnace will receive a farther supply. The whole quantity of sand put in at one smelting measures 617 cubical inches, and weighs, when dry, about 42½ lb. avoirdupois. This gives a mass of iron, which, when forged, makes 11 wedges, each intended to make a 'ploughshare', and weighing fully 1 82/100 lb. The workmen here, therefore, procure from the ore about 47 per cent. of malleable iron; but, as usual in India, their iron is very impure."

As regards mining in areas around the present-day Chitradurga district, Buchanan mentioned about places such as *Cudera Canavay, Buca Sagurada Canavay* and *Doda Rashy Guda.* He also referred to a place called *Ellady-caray* in *Heriuru* (Hiriyur) where smelting works had been discontinued long back owing to shortage of fuel (May 2, 1801).

> "**Iron**. - Iron was formerly smelted in *Ellady-caray* from black sand, which was brought from a hill about two miles to the westward. Much of the *vitreous scoriae* remains where the furnaces stood; but the work has been abandoned these sixty years; the want of fewel is indeed a sufficient reason."

From the above descriptions given by Buchanan, it is revealed that enormous quantities of charcoal were required for smelting iron ore. Apparently, all the tree growth occurring in the forest lands around the iron smelting sites was cleared for the preparation of charcoal. In Buchanan's own words 'The fuel used is charcoal prepared from any kind of tree that grows in the country, except the *Ficus Bengalensis*, and the *Chloroxylon Dupada* of my manuscripts.' [Buchanan; Vol. II, Page No. 20.] Buchanan had also mentioned about the use of bamboo charcoal for further purification of the iron rendering it fit for being wrought up into the implements of husbandry, when the iron is repeatedly put in furnace. Firewood (charcoal) played such a crucial role in the iron smelting industry that sometimes smelting operation had to be given up with the exhaustion of firewood (charcoal) in the nearby areas, as transportation of either charcoal or iron ore over longer distances to the site of the furnace (forge) was an economically unviable proposition, making the final product, namely, iron prohibitively costly.

MANUFACTURE OF STEEL

Manufacture of steel also required large quantities of charcoal. The process of making steel in Magadi, as narrated by Buchanan on 13th June, 1800 is as below.

"**Steel**. - The same persons also make steel. Good clay is mixed with an equal quantity of the charcoal that is made from *Paddy* husks; and, having been well moistened with water, is thoroughly mixed, by being trodden under the feet of oxen. It is then picked clean, and made into cuppels, which are dried one day in the shade, and the next day in the sun. A fire place is then made, in form of a parallelogram, by placing two stones one cubit long, and two inches and a half high, parallel to each other. At the distance of a foot above the stones is placed a wall of clay eight inches high. One end is shut up, in the same manner, by stone and clay; the other is built up with clay alone to the height of two cubits. Through this is inserted a tube for two bellows. Each of the cuppels is now loaded with a small piece of iron, from one to one and a half *Seer* (9 3/10 *oz.* to 14 *oz.*) in weight together with five small pieces of the *Tangayree* wood (*Cassia auriculata*). Three rows of the loaded cuppels are placed one above the other, so as to occupy the whole area of the furnace; the room of one cuppel only being left empty, opposite to the muzzle of the bellows, in order to give access to the wind. They are covered with two bushels of charcoal, and burned for six hours; a third bushel of charcoal having been added, as the former two were consumed. The pieces are then taken out, and hammered into small square bars, having been heated with charcoal of the *Sujalu* (*Mimosa Tuggula*, Buch. MSS.)"

[**Note**: Present name of *Mimosa Tuggula* is *Albizia amara*]

In his diaries, Buchanan had also narrated the process of steel making in the mining areas which now come under Tumkur district (August 13, 1800). A portion of his narration is reproduced below.

"The crucibles are made, in a conical form, of unbaked clay, and each would contain about a pint of water. In each is put one third part of a wedge of iron, with three *Rupees* weight (531 grains) of the stem of the *Tayngada* or *Cassia auriculata*, and two green leaves of the *Huginay*, which is no doubt a *Convolvulus*, or an *Ipomea* with a large smooth leaf; but never having seen the flower, I could not in such a difficult class of plants attempt to ascertain the species. The mouth of the crucible is then covered with a round cap of unbaked clay, and the junction is well luted. The crucibles, thus loaded, are well dried near the fire, and are then fit for the furnace.----"

[**Note:** Buchanan had not indicated the specific reason for adding the plant parts of *Cassia auriculata* and a few other species to the iron. It is believed that these were added in order to increase the carbon content in the steel resulting in the formation of beautiful patterns. This technology originated in the mid-1st millennium BC in present day Tamil Nadu, then spread across the rest of peninsular India, and was also exported globally. The product was known as Wootz steel. It also came to be known as Wootz Damascus steel, as the south Indian technology had spread to the city of Damascus in Syria and led to the development of a steel industry around the city that specialized in making weapons (swords) of this steel. The origin of the word 'wootz' probably lies in the south Indian words for steel – ehku (Tamil), ukku (Kannada and Telugu) and urukk (Malayalam).]

GLASS INDUSTRY

In Mysore State, glass was manufactured in two places. In Channapatna, glass bottles and ornamental rings (bangles) were manufactured. Glass bangles of five colours (black, red, blue, green and yellow) were also manufactured in a place called *Muteodu* in present Chitradurga district.

The main source of energy for the furnaces was charcoal. Firewood was also used in certain processes.

TEXTILE INDUSTRY

During his long halt at Bangalore (22nd June to 2nd July, 1800), Buchanan had made detailed enquiries about various economic activities pursued by the people. In order to know about the manufacture of cloth, he obtained the relevant details from an assembly of different kinds of weavers. While the information provided by Buchanan was very detailed, his observations with regard to the use of plant-products in the textile industry will only be discussed briefly in the following paragraphs.

Plant-products were used in the textile industry mainly as dyeing agents. For dyeing silk with red colour, the principal ingredient was *Lac*, with a small quantity of *Ludo* bark, and a little turmeric. These were mixed with soda and then boiled in water. Boiling was repeated a number of times by adding more water to the decoction. The silk was first immersed in an infusion of tamarind (kept in water for two days), and heated until it was too hot for the hand. The silk was then removed, the decoction of *Lac* added to the tamarind infusion, and the silk was again put to this mixture and boiled for three hours. If the colour of silk was perfect, nothing more was to be done. If it was darker than required, some tamarind infusion was added to make it lighter. If it was lighter, some more *Lac* decoction was added to arrive at the right color. In some places, cochineal was also used to get the red colour, but it was quite expensive. [**Note**: The source of the *Lodu* bark was not mentioned.]

For dyeing silk in pale orange colour, the dyeing agent used was *Capili Podi*, or dust collected from the flowers of *Rotleria tinctoria* (present name *Wrightia tinctoria* – hale/beppale). Other ingredients were Sesamum oil, soda, *Suja Cara* (another type of soda), a small quantity of alum, and water. For dyeing silk in yellow, the dyeing agent was turmeric, the remaining ingredients being the same as above. If the yellow silk was dyed in indigo, then immersed in an infusion of tamarind and dried in the shade, it resulted in a fine green colour.

For dying cotton threads in red colour, the principal dyeing agent was the powdered bark of the root of the *Muddi* (two species of *Morinda*, namely, *Morinda citrifolia* and *Morinda ternifolia*). The other ingredients were powdered soda, sheep's dung, Sesamum oil, and water.

To dye cotton thread green, the thread was first dyed to a sky blue (*Mavi*) colour with indigo, and then put in water containing powdered turmeric and five *Myrobalans* (fruit of *Terminalia chebula*) powdered and juice of ten limes.

Cotton cloth was dyed to a fine red colour resembling that of the pomegranate flower, called *Gulenari* for which the main ingredient used was the *Cossumba*, or the flowers of the *Carthamus tinctorius* (safflower). Since the demand for the *Cossumba* dye was higher than its supply, *Cossumba* powder was often adulterated with the powdered flowers of the *Yecada*, or *Asclepias gigantea* (present name *Calotropis gigantea* – ekke). This resulted in an ordinary red colour. For getting the true *Gulenari* colour, the decoction of the best quality *cossumba* powder was mixed with the powder of *Tundu* flowers (*Cedrela toona*).

Cotton thread or cotton cloth was dyed to a very dark blue colour (almost black) by repeated immersions in indigo followed by sprinkling of a decoction of the bark of *Swamy*, or *Swietenia febrifuga* (present name *Soymida febrifuga*).

The silk-weavers were known as *Puttuegars* who themselves did the work of dyeing their silk. The cotton weavers belonged to three communities: the *Shayanagaru*, the *Kannada Devangas*, and the *Teliga Devangas*. They also dyed their cloths and threads themselves except when they bought red thread from places across the Krishna River. A community called *Nilagaru* monopolized the profession of dyeing blue (with indigo); they used to get work from the other communities mentioned above as and when necessary.

In addition to dyeing of cloth, printing of cotton cloth was also in vogue. Printing was done by a set of people called *Rungaru*. They used to print in two colours, red and black. The work of readying the cotton cloth for printing was fairly elaborate involving a number of ingredients such as sheep's dung, quick lime, *Myrobalans* (fruit of *Terminalia chebula*), gum of the *Dinduga* tree (*Andersonia Panchmoum*, Roxb. MSS. - Present name *Anogeissus latifolia*), etc. The *Mordant* for red dye was prepared with alum, *dinduga* gum and water. The *Mordant* for black dye consisted of a number of ingredients such as iron dross, old iron, *kanji* (decoction of rice), sugar-jagory, ghee (boiled butter) and *dinduga* gum.

Buchanan mentioned that the *Rangarus* dyed cotton cloth to a bright red colour for which they used a wood called *Patunga* along with other ingredients such as alum and powdered *Myrobalans* (fruit of *Terminalia chebula*). The scientific name of the Patunga wood was not indicated.

Buchanan also mentioned that to prepare the indigo dye, the *Nilagarus* took indigo, ground with a little water to a fine powder, put it into a pot containing water, added a decoction of *Tagashay Bija*, or seed of the *Cassia tora*. The above decoction was prepared by boiling the *Cassia tora* seeds in water and adding soda, quick-lime and pot-ash. The pot-ash was prepared by burning branches of the *Kalli* (*Euphorbium tirucalli*), or of the *Utrayena* (*Achyranthes muricata*) (present name *Achyranthes aspera* – uttarani/aparmaga).

Indigenous production of Silk

During the time of Buchanan's visit to Mysore and Canara, silk was imported, there being no indigenous production of this prized commodity. Tipu Sultan had made some attempt at planting mulberry plants but there was not much progress. Buchanan had assessed that the climate of Mysore was quite ideal for growing mulberry. In that distant past, he had foreseen a great potential of silk production in the Mysore State through propagation of mulberry plants. His prophetic observations in this regard are remarkable. [Buchanan Vol. I. Chapter IV, Page No. 222.]

> "**Silk manufacture**. – The silk manufacture seems especially favourable for a country so far from the sea, and from navigable rivers: as long carriage, on such a valuable article, is of little importance. At present all the raw material is imported: but I see no reason why it might not be raised in *Mysore* to great advantage. *Tippoo* had commenced a trial, but his arbitrary measures were little calculated to ensure success. Some of the mulberry trees, however, that remain in his gardens, show how well the plant agrees with the climate. It is true, that the experiments hitherto tried below the

Ghats have not been favourable; but much resolution and patience are always required to introduce any new article of cultivation; and I suspect that the climate here, owing to its being more temperate, will be found more favourable than that of the lower *Carnatic*."

LEATHER INDUSTRY (TANNING)

Buchanan gave a fairly comprehensive account of the process of tanning of animal skins to make leather; tanning was done by a community of people called *Madigaru*. A number of plant-products were used for the purpose of tanning. Buchanan's observations are reproduced below.

"**Goat and sheep skins tanning**. – To dress the raw hides of sheep or goats, the *Madigaru* in the first place wash them clean, and then rub each with the fourth part of a kind of soft paste, made of 6 *Dudus* weight of the milky juice of the *Yecada* (*Asclepias gigantea*), about 6 *Dudus* weight (2 426/1000 ounces) of salt (muriate of soda), and twelve *Dudus* weight of *Ragy Sanguty*, or pudding of the *Cynosurus coracanus*, with a sufficient quantity of water. This paste is rubbed on the hairy side, and the skins are then exposed for three days to the sun; after which they are washed with water, beating them well on a stone, as is usual in this country. This takes off the hair. Then powder 2 *Seers* (1 213/1000 *lb.*) of *Arulay Myrobalans* (fruit of *Terminalia chebula*) and put them and one skin into a pot with 3 or 4 *Seers* measure of hot water, where it is to remain for three days. The skin is then to be washed and dried.

"**Black skins**. – This tanned skin is dyed black as follows: take of old iron, and of the dross of iron forges, each a handful, of plantain and lime-skins, each five or six; put them into a pot with some *Ragy kanji*, or decoction of *Ragy*, and let them stand for eight days. Then rub the liquor on the skins, which immediately become black.

"**Red skins**. – These skins may be dyed red by the following process: Take of ungarbled *Lac* 2 *Dudus* weight (about 13 drams), of *suja cara*, or fine soda, 1 *Dudu* weight, and of *Ludo* bark 2 *Dudus* weight.

Having taken the sticks from the *Lac*, and powdered the soda and bark, boil them all together in a *Seer* of water (68 3/8 cubical inches) for 1½ hour. Rub the skin, after it has been freed from the hair as before mentioned, with this decoction; and then put it into the pot with the *Myrobalans* (fruit of *Terminalia chebula*) and water for three days. This is a good colour, and for many purposes the skins are well dressed.

"**Neat hides**. – The hides of oxen and buffaloes are dressed as follows: For each skin take two *Seers* (1 213/1000 lb.) of quick lime, and 5 or 6 *Seers* measure (about 1 1/3 ale gallon) of water; and in this mixture keep the skins for eight days, and rub off the hair. Then for each skin take ten *Seers*, by weight, (about 6 lb.) of the unpeeled sticks of the *Tayngadu* (*Cassia auriculata*), and 10 *Seers* measure of water (about 2½ ale gallons), and in this infusion keep the skins for four days. For an equal length of time, add the same quantity of *Tayngadu* and water. Then wash, and dry the skins in the sun, stretching them out with pegs. This leather is very bad."

[**Note:** Buchanan had not provided the scientific name of the plant from which the *Ludo* bark was extracted. Fruit of *Terminalia chebula* was mainly used as *Myrobalan*]

AGRO-PROCESSING INDUSTRIES

Processing of Areca nut

When camping at Madhugiri during the period from 25th July to 29th July, 1800, Buchanan had made enquiries about various aspects including agricultural practices being adopted in Madhugiri and surrounding areas. Buchanan was informed that, the bark of the Babul or Karijali (*Acacia nilotica/arabica*) tree and *Cut* or *Terra Japonica* (a product of *Acacia catechu* tree) were used in the processing of areca nut. Buchanan described the entire process as follows.

"-----. The nut, after being peeled, is cut into seven or eight pieces, and put up in a heap. Then take one *Seer* of the nut, one *Seer* of

Cut, or *Terra Japonica*, and a hundred leaves of the *Piper Betel*, beat them together repeatedly with some water, and strain the juice thus obtained into a pot. Take 20 *Seers* of the bark of the *Cari Jali* (*Mimosa indica* E. M.), and boil it during a whole night in a large pot, with forty *Seers* of water. With this decoction mix the juice expressed from the former materials, and boil them. While it is boiling, put in the *Areca* nut, after it has been cut, until the pot be full. Immediately after, take it out with a ladle, put in more, till the whole is boiled. In order to be dried, it must be three days exposed on mats to the sun, and is then fit for sale.---"

The processing of areca nut in the *Ghat* areas was somewhat different. Buchanan provided the following information regarding processing of areca nut in and around Sirsi (March 15, 1801) as follows.

"The crop season of an *Areca* garden continues from two months before, till one after, the winter solstice. The bunches are cut as they approach to ripeness, for the ripe nut is of no use except for seed. The husk is removed with a knife. A decoction is then made with a few nuts, a little *Chunam* (ashes of the bark of the *Chuncoa Muttia* Buch. MSS.), and some bark of the *Honay*, or *Pterocarpus santalinus*. These are bruised together and boiled six hours in water. A quantity of the nut cleared from the husk is then put in a pot, and into this the decoction is poured, until it rises above the nuts, which are then boiled till the eyes separate. They are now put upon a strainer of mats supported on posts, and are dried six days in the sun. At night they are covered with a mat. In this country the *Betel-nut* is never cut, but is sold entire, and is called red *Betel*. Any nuts of a bunch, that have become too ripe before it was cut, are picked out and kept separate. Their husks are removed, and they are dried in the sun without boiling. These are called raw *Betel*, and sell much lower than the other kind."

[**Note**: The present name of *Chuncoa Muttia* is *Terminalia tomentosa* (matti) and that of *Honay* is *Pterocarpus marsupium*.]

Other agro-processing activities

Most of the agro-processing activities required substantial quantities of firewood for the purpose of boiling/heating. Certain specific timber (hard and heavy) such as that of *Schleichera oleosa* (kusum/sagade) was used for oil pressing and also in sugar industry.

Bark of Matti (*Terminalia tomentosa*) as a source of lime

The use of the bark of the matti tree as a source of lime was not only restricted to the processing of areca-nut, but it was also used for other purposes. In this context, the following observations of Buchanan which he made during his tour of Sirsi are reproduced below.

> ***Strata of Jaydi Munnu.*** – In low moist vallies here, a kind of white clay, mixed with small bits of quartz, is commonly found under the soil of rice-grounds. Its *strata* are often several cubits in thickness, and, where it comes to the surface, render the ground very sterile. It is called *Jaydi Munnu*, and is used to white-wash the houses of the natives. It is diffused in water to separate the sand and stones, and is then mixed with a little *Chunam*, that is to say, the ashes of the Muddi bark (*Chuncoa Muddia* Buch. MSS.); for in this vicinity there is no lime."

DISTILLATION OF SPIRITUOUS LIQUOR

In *Chapter 5* it has been mentioned that Buchanan had come across the tree *Elate sylvestris* (present name *Phoenix sylvestris* – ichalu) on many occasions during his tour. Buchanan had described the tree in detail because of the widespread presence of the tree in Mysore and also due to the fact that excise duty on spirituous liquor was an important source of revenue to the government. Although Tipu Sultan was against people drinking spirituous liquor and had ordered removal of these trees, the practice of making toddy and Jagory from the tree was prevalent perhaps because it was not possible to do away with such a potential source of revenue. Besides, toddy-tapping was an important profession providing employment to many people.

Apparently, Tipu's orders were implemented only in the areas surrounding Srirangapatna; elsewhere, it was business as usual.

While camping at Malur (*Waluru*) on 7th May, 1800, on way to Srirangapatna via Bangalore, Buchanan visited the house of a distiller in order to have firsthand information about the process involved in the preparation of spirituous liquor. While observing the process of distillation, Buchanan noticed that the bark of the tree *Acacia leucophloea* (bilijali) was an important ingredient used in the distillation.

> **"Distilled spirits**. - In the evening I went to the house of a distiller of country rum, in order to examine his process. The bark of the *Mimosa leucophlea* Roxb: is considered as a necessary ingredient. This tree grows commonly in the country, and is called *Cari Jaly* in the *Canarese, Nella tumica* in the *Telinga*, and *Caru velun* in the *Tamul*. The bark is dried, and cut into chips, of which about four pounds are added to one *maund* (24¼ lb.) of sugar-cane *Jagory*, with a quantity of water equal to about twice the bulk of this sweet substance. The mixture is made in an earthen jar, which is kept in the shade, and the fermentation commences in about twenty-four hours. It is completed on the twelfth day; when the liquor is distilled by the following apparatus (see Figure in next page). The body of the still (a a a) is a strong earthen jar, capable of containing three times the bulk of the materials. On this is luted, with cow dung, a copper head (b b b), having on the inside a gutter (c c) for collecting the vapour that has been condensed into spirit by a constant small stream of water, which falls on the head (f). This water is conveyed away by the pipe (g), while the spirit is conducted into a jar by the pipe (d). The mode of condensing the spirit is very rude; and the liquor, which is never rectified by a second distillation, is execrable. The natives allege that the bark, which is very insipid to the taste, is useful, by diminishing the too great sweetness of the *Jagory*. To me, however, it appears to be rather of use by regulating the fermentation; which, in such a warm climate, would be apt to run suddenly into the acetous."

[**Note:** In the above description, Buchanan had given the Kannada name of *Mimosa leucophlea* Roxb: (present name *Acacia leucophloea*) as *Cari Jaly* (*Kari jali*). However, in Kannada language the words *Bili Jali* are used for *Acacia leucophloea*, which is reasonable, as the word leuco means white (Bily). The words *Kari Jali, Gobli* (*Babul* in Hindi) are actually used for another species *Acacia arabica/nilotica*. Traditionally, the bark of *Bili Jali* or *Acacia leucophloea* was used in the distillation of toddy.]

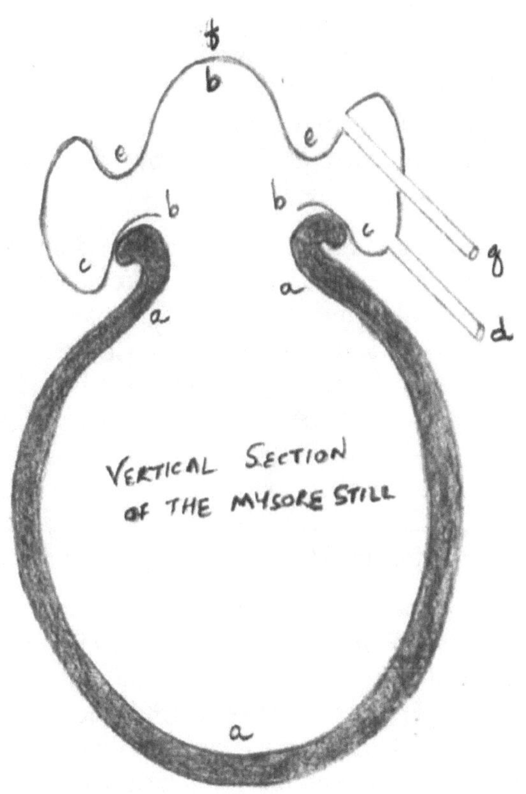

CHANNAPATNA (*CHINAPATAM*)

During the time of Buchanan's visit in 1800-01, Channapatna was an important town of Mysore State. Coco-nut, betel-nut and sugar-cane were three important crops grown around the town. It was known for the manufacture of sugar and jaggery. There was a sugar-mill in the town. Buchanan also mentioned about a family of *Linga Banijigaru* who had the art of making very fine white sugar. 'The process has always been kept a profound secret by the head of the house, who instructs his successor only before his death.' This sugar was made for the exclusive use of the court (i.e. the royal family).

Channapatna was also an important industrial town for the manufacture of glass-ware and steel-wire. Ornamental rings (coloured bangles) and small bottles were two important glass-ware products of the town. Steel-wire manufactured at Channapatna was used for the strings of musical instruments.

Forests around Channapatna abounded with the trees of *Wrightia tinctoria* (hale). Bulk of the Mysore State's requirement of the *Capily Podi* dye, which was sourced from the flowers of the hale tree, was supplied from these forests. *Wrightia tinctoria* was also an important timber tree of the region. Buchanan had mentioned about the utility of the tree which he had seen at Bidadi as follows: 'Grows sometimes to a large tree, and is used for planks.' He had seen a tree of the same species in the forests of Savana-durga, and described its utility as follows: "The natives are acquainted with its dyeing quality. Its timber is said to be hard, and white like ivory, and is used for small furniture, such as beds and chairs."

It is likely that due to high demand in the past from the textile industry for the *Capily Podi* dye, people were consciously protecting the trees to ensure sustained supply of the dye, and only large trees were harvested for timber. However, with the introduction of synthetic dyes, demand for the *Kapily Podi* dye must have come down, which resulted in people harvesting younger trees also for their timber needs. Availability of large numbers of small and medium sized hale trees must have given tremendous boost to the toy-making industry for which Channapatna town eventually became very famous. Nowadays one hardly comes across a *Wrightia tinctoria* tree of a size capable of giving any timber for furniture. In fact the hale wood is now so scarcely available that people sell the wood to the artisans (toymakers) by weight instead of by volume.

Chapter 9

FORESTS OF MYSORE STATE

Buchanan had undertaken a fairly long journey in the Mysore State covering various regions. His focus during the journey was to acquaint himself with the overall economic, social and cultural conditions of the state and her people, and to apprise the Government by submitting a comprehensive report. He devoted a substantial part of his journey in apprising himself of the agricultural and economic activities of the state. Being an accomplished botanist, he was naturally drawn towards trees and other plants as and when he came across them during his travel. But he kept his interest in them limited to knowing about their utility in agricultural, economic or other purposes. Besides, during that time the concept of forest as an administrative unit or as an ecological entity had not yet developed. Land harboring natural vegetation was generally termed as wasteland except when it was populated by valuable trees of impressive growth. At times, even well-wooded lands used to be called wastelands if the trees were of no economic use. Quite often, cultivated lands and natural wastelands used to get interchanged. During his tour, Buchanan came across large extents of land which had been cultivated in the past but were subsequently turned into wastelands, having been abandoned by the cultivators due to various reasons such as wars, invasions, epidemics, droughts, famines, exorbitantly heavy tax burdens, etc.

Fortunately, during his journey, Buchanan had passed through some good natural forests, where he took interest in identifying the trees and in ascertaining their uses. In addition, oftentimes during his travel, Buchanan made it a point to describe the appearance of the country that he was passing through. His narrations invariably included one or two sentences about the natural vegetation of the landscape. In case the vegetation included some species of economic importance or of some significance for other reasons, he would describe them in more detail. Such bits of information help in assessing the status of natural vegetation or forest in the area.

In his narrations Buchanan used different terminologies to indicate the status of tree growth. The terminology 'forest' was usually reserved for trees with impressive growth. In case the trees were not known to be of any importance or use, the phrase 'useless forest' was often used. The terminology 'wood' was generally used to indicate trees with noticeable growth. Low trees or stunted trees were meant for forest with poor to mediocre growth. The phrase 'copse wood' was used to indicate savanna type of growth where scattered groups of small trees dominated the scene. The terminology shrub was used to indicate short scrub-type vegetation.

In the following paragraphs, we will highlight some of the observations that Buchanan had made regarding the surrounding natural vegetation as he visited different parts of Mysore State. Based on these observations, an attempt will be made to visualize an image of how the forests of the Mysore State had looked like during the beginning of the nineteenth century.

Natural vegetation from Bethamangala to Srirangapatna

The first leg of Buchanan's journey in the Mysore State started from near Bethamangala and ended at Srirangapatna. He travelled through the present districts of Kolar (southern part), Bengaluru Rural (small portion), Bengaluru Urban, Ramanagara and Mandya. This phase of Buchanan's journey was by and large through fairly barren countryside with pockets of poor to stunted natural vegetation; towards the end of this phase, he had seen some moderate to good forests around Bidadi and Channapatna.

Greater part of the terrain between Bethamangala and Tekal (*Tayculum*) consisted of high rocky hills, the remainder being covered with copse woods chiefly of *Albizia amara* (tugli) trees. Between Tekal and Malur, most of the area was covered with brush or copse wood and no large timber trees; although in some places the trees grew to a size sufficient for building rural houses and other country purposes. The brush woods, in most places, were low and consisted chiefly of *Cassia auriculata* and *Ptelea viscosa* (present name *Dodonaea viscosa*) which according to Buchanan were the most common bushes throughout this part of the country. Around Kadugodi (*Catcolli*), the wasteland contained much low brush wood, in some places intermixed with stunted *mimosas* (present name *Acacias*). Between Kadugodi and Bangalore also, Buchanan found the countryside naked where six tenths appeared to be arable, the remainder being covered with low bushes, and much of it seemed capable of being brought into cultivation. Buchanan had also found the area to be better pasture land. Between Bangalore to Kengeri, the uncultivated land was hilly, hillier than what Buchanan had seen in the Mysore territory so far. It was also very rocky and bare, even copse wood being absent.

While approaching Bidadi (*Wiridy* or *Biridy*), Buchanan had noticed some change in the vegetation of the landscape from being one of 'continued copse' to 'some small villages scattered in the woods'. At Bidadi, for the first time in the Mysore State, Buchanan came across trees of noticeable growth that he termed as woods, describing as follows:

> **"Woods** - The uncultivated land is very hilly, and in many places rocky; yet some of it seems capable of being rendered arable. Except for fewel, the wood is of very little use, as it is in general too small for planks, or beams. Tigers are numerous among the copse; a circumstance, however, which does not prevent the inhabitants from sending their cattle into it. A beast is occasionally lost; but this loss is compensated by the abundance of grass. The woods here are not impenetrable, like those of *Chittagong*, where a luxuriant growth of rattans, and climbers of numerous kinds, prevents all ingress. Here every thing is stunted, and the trees serve to render the grass better, by sheltering it from the sun."

During his halt at Bidadi for a day (13th May, 1800), Buchanan had gone to the nearby woods for his evening walk when a number of trees were shown to him as being useful. The trees were:

1. *Mara halaya* (*Nerium tinctorium*, Rox.);

2. *Mara haralu* (*Iatropha curcas*, Lin.);

3. *Alaygara* (*Terminalia myrobalana citrina* of *Koenig.*);

4. *Devadarum* (*Erythroxylon sideroxyloides* of *Lamarck*.);

5. *Sri Gunda Chica* (*Santalum album, Lin.*);

6. *Wotu* (*Loranthus falcatus, Lin.*);

7. *Easy* (*Premna tomentosa*, Willd.);

8. *Ha-Shi-Cai* (*Mimosa pennata.*); and

9. *Cacay* (Cassia *fistula, Lin.*).

On the next day, Buchanan came across a forest with fairly good growth of trees near Channapatna. He described the forest as follows:

> "**Forests. 14**[th] **May**. – I went to *Chinapatam*, or *Chinapatana*, through a very beautiful country, consisting of swelling grounds, in some places cultivated, and in many more covered with trees, which are intermixed with steep fantastic rocks and hills. The trees here are by far the finest that I have seen in either *Carnatic*, although they fall very short of the stately forests of *Chittagong*. In these woods the *bamboo* is common. It is now in flower, and produces a great quantity of grain, which is gathered for food by the poor inhabitants of the neighbourhood."

Buchanan had found most of the areas between Channapatna and Maddur to be arable except some high hills separating these two places. Most of the areas were in a state of nature, and were covered with brushwood. As regards the terrain surrounding Mandya, Buchanan had opined that although the country was free from hills and about half of the area was arable, much of it could be rendered arable without difficulty, though the soil was in general poor. The wasteland was occupied by brushwood, and many places were covered with the *Phoenix farinifera* among which were some trees of wild date (*Elate sylvestris*). Buchanan had noted that half of the areas between Mandya to Srirangapatna were free from rocks or wastelands; the remaining half was a hilly country, stony and bare, about which Buchanan had commented thus: 'From ascending the ridge, until reaching the *Cavery*, one can hardly find a bush sufficiently large to make a broom.'

Savana-durga forests in Magadi

During the next phase of his journey, Buchanan left Srirangapatna on 6th June, 1800 for Bangalore. Initially, his route was the same by which he had earlier travelled from Bangalore to Srirangapatna. However, after Channapatna, he took a deviation at Ramanagara (*Rama-giri)* and proceeded towards Magadi. Buchanan described the face of the country near Magadi as follows:

> **"June 13. Face of the country**. - I went to *Magadi*, which in our maps is called *Maghery*. This stage was very fatiguing for my cattle; and the road passed through a wild but romantic country, which consists of low hills, intermixed with little cultivated vallies. The soil of these is tolerably good; and, like the *Rama-giri* valley, they are cultivated with dry grains only. The higher parts are covered with trees, which, owing to the poverty of the soil, are in most places very small; but near *Savana-durga*, and in a few other parts, the timber and *Bamboos* grow to a good size. The summits of all the ridges of hills are bare rocks of the granitic porphyry, and often rise into high sharp peaks, or immense masses of naked stone. By far the most remarkable of these is occupied by *Savana-durga*, which the army of Lord Cornwallis took by assault; ever since which time it has been deserted."

On 15th June, Buchanan visited part of the Savana-durga forests and described as follows:

> "In the hollow ground near the river are some of the best forests in the country, the trees growing to a considerable size. The cattle of the inhabitants never go into them; nor can any one cut the timber without an order from government. Much of the lower land in this forest might be cleared and cultivated."

Buchanan had spent more number of days at Magadi (up to June 19, 1800), sharing his time between visiting iron ore mines and forges, and collecting specimens of trees from the Savana-durga forests. On the basis of his observations of the tree specimens and information elicited from the local people, Buchanan described the tree species along with their principal uses and other characteristics. The list of trees comprising seventy (70) species along with Buchanan's narration/comments has been appended at **Annexure I.**

On 20th June, Buchanan proceeded to Tavarekere 'by a road passing the whole way through woods'. On 21st June, as Buchanan proceeded to Bangalore, he described the face of the country as follows:

> **"June 21. Face of the country.** – I went from *Taveri-caray* to *Bangalore*. Much of the country is covered with bushes, and consists of a very poor soil. The greater part of the arable lands near *Bangalore* are cultivated: but at some distance from it many fields are waste, owing to a want of people."

Natural vegetation from Bangalore to Kolar, Chikkaballapur, Doddaballapur, Madhugiri, Sira, Chikkanayakanahalli, Nagamangala and other places

After halting at Bangalore for ten days, Buchanan had set out for a long journey on 3rd July, 1800, for almost two months, returning to Srirangapatna on 1st September, 1800. He travelled through towns and villages situated in the present districts of Bengaluru Urban, Kolar, Chikkaballapur, Bengaluru Rural, Tumkur and Mandya.

Buchanan travelled to Malur via Agara and Sarjapur through a country much of which consisted of wasteland that was remarkably bare. From Malur to Vakkaleri, half of the way passed through a barren country thinly covered with bushes and stunted trees. Beyond this there was gradual improvement in the soil and the areas were well cultivated and well-wooded. Between Vakkaleri and Kolar, the first part of the road passed through a narrow valley, confined between two ridges of low, rocky, naked hills. The valley in many places was formerly cultivated and then abandoned turning the area into wasteland, being covered with bushes, among which the *Oleander* (*Nerium odorum*) was common. Farther on, with the hills to the right disappearing, the country in that direction was level to a great extent, seemed to be very fertile, and had probably once been almost all cultivated. Between Kolar and *Calura* (probably Kaiwara), the country contained many detached, naked, rocky hills, the mist frequently resting on top of the hills, while the country below was clear. Between *Calura* and Sidlaghatta, a great part of the country was overgrown with stunted bushes, even where the soil appeared to be tolerably good, and had never been cultivated. In this portion, the number of rocky hills came down considerably. While travelling from Sidlaghatta to Chikkaballapur, Buchanan had noticed that the entire area was arable but a great part of it having been uninhabited had become wasteland.

When travelling from Chikkaballapur to Bidikere located by the side of Nandi-durga, Buchanan passed through a number of hills including the Nandi hills which represent the highest part in the central region of Mysore State, being the source of a number of rivers such as *Pennar* and *Palar*. With regard to the vegetation of the Nandi hills, Buchanan had mentioned as follows:

> "Among the hills *Nandi-durga* is much fertile land, now covered with *Bamboos*, and useless trees; but which, with little encouragement, might be brought into cultivation:----"

Buchanan had noticed that most of the country between Bidikere and Doddaballapur which had been formerly cultivated was almost entirely unoccupied. Between Doddaballapur and Tondebavi (*Tonday Bava* - near *Maha-kali-durga*), the country was chiefly barren and hilly, totally uncultivated, and covered with bushes or coppice wood. Between Tondebavi (*Tonday Bava*) and *Assaruru*, the country was level, but contained several ridges of barren hills. It was intersected by the channels of several mountain torrents, which were wide and full of sand; but even during the monsoon season when Buchanan had passed through (21st July), they contained no water. Buchanan had been informed that after heavy rains they were full only for a little while. Between *Assaruru* and *Doddabailea*, most of the areas were cultivated earlier and were covered with bushes and coppice wood. The terrain between *Doddabailea* and Madhugiri was surrounded by rocky and bare hills interspersed with fertile valleys. Between Madhugiri and Badavanahalli, the valleys were interspersed with detached barren hills. There were good cultivated lands where cultivation had been given up and the areas were colonized by *Elate sylvestris*. Between Badavanahalli and Sira, greater part of the country was covered with trees, which were rather higher than what were usual in the wastes of the country. Among them were many wild date palms (*Elate sylvestris*). Although Tipu Sultan had directed removal of the wild date palm trees, his direction did not appear to have been obeyed; Buchanan had commented thus: 'Like most of his regulations, this seems to have been very ill obeyed; for in the central parts of his dominions no tree seems to be in such abundance.'

From Sira, Buchanan had travelled to *Madigheshi* (8th August, 1800) in the Nizam's territories. On the way, he had noticed that the greater part of the country was covered with low trees, but much of it was fit for cultivation. The country around *Madigheshi* was full of little hills, and was overgrown with copse wood. Buchanan returned to Madhugiri on 10th August, 1800, through pretty valleys surrounded by detached rocky hills. These valleys exhibited signs of having been cultivated in a great measure and contained the ruins of the villages of the previous inhabitants. Ever since the depredation committed by the Marathas, and the subsequent famine, these lands had turned waste, and many of the fields were overgrown with young trees.

From Madhugiri, Buchanan proceeded towards Tumkur via Thovinakere, visiting on the way some mining and smelting sites near *Chin-narayan-durga*, where the country, for the most part, consisted of a rugged valley surrounded by hills. Buchanan found the terrain around Tumkur fairly level: 'The country is the most level, and the freest from rocks, of any that I have yet seen above the *Ghats*. I observed only one place in which the granite showed itself above the surface. The soil in most places is good, and might be entirely cultivated. Near *Tavina-Caray* it is so; but as I approached *Tumcuru*, I observed more and more waste land.' Buchanan was somewhat disappointed at not having come across good wooded land around Tumkur despite the fact that the terrain harbored good soil: 'At some distance on my left were hills; and the prospect would have been very beautiful, had the country been better wooded; but, except for some palm gardens scattered at great distances, it has very few trees'. While moving on to Gubbi, Buchanan passed through almost similar landscape: 'The country, between *Tumcuru* and *Gubi*, consists of gently swelling lands, entirely resembling that through which I came yesterday. A very considerable proportion of it is not cultivated'. The terrain continued to be similar as Buchanan proceeded further towards *Muga-nayakana-cotay* and then to *Conli*. As Buchanan approached *Conli*, he made the following observations highlighting the peculiarities of the terrain of this part of Mysore State.

"17th August. – In the morning I went two and a half cosses to *Conli*. About three miles from my last night's quarters, the country is hilly; but the hills are lower, and not near so rugged as those to the eastward among the *Durgas*. Owing probably to the vicinity of the iron mines, they are very bare of trees, and their surface is covered with small stones intermixed with bare rock; but this, not being granite, never appears in those immense naked masses so common in the hills running north from *Capala-durga*, or near the eastern *Ghats*. The hills here, as well as the others above the *Ghats*, do not form long uninterrupted ridges, but are almost every where surrounded by level ground; so that in travelling among them, there is little occasion to ascend any great heights. The vallies in some places are narrow, and torn up by the empty channels of torrents; in other places they are wide, and well-cultivated. I am informed, that this range of low hills extends all the way north to *Chatrakal*, and in its course comes near to *Sira*. It seems to extend about three miles south from *Conli*; and beyond that I can see quite a level country, extending to a low range of hills at *Miasamudra*.---"

Buchanan spent a few days examining iron ore mines and quarries of other minerals in the surrounding areas including those at Chikkanayakanahalli. He had also visited a temple at *Malaiswara* located atop a hillock near a village named *Madana Mada* (August 19, 1800). Buchanan had noticed some tree growth above the temple, which he described as follows:

"The temple of *Malaiswara* is a very poor building; but is much frequented at a festival in the month of *Magha*. Some of the figures on the chariot of the image are exceedingly indecent. The woods above the temple are rather taller than usual in these barren hills, and contain many trees of the *Dupada, Chloroxylon Dupada,* Buch: MSS. The resin is used as incense; and musical instruments, somewhat resembling the guitar, are made of the wood. From the top of the hill the view is very fine; the country being composed of hills, cultivated fields, reservoirs like small lakes, and palm gardens, all intermixed. --- ."

[**Note:** The present name of *Chloroxylon Dupada* is *Boswellia serrata*]

From Chikkanayakanahalli, Buchanan proceeded to Aralaguppe (*Arulu Gupay*) and further onward to Turuvekere (*Turiva-Caray*). Towards Aralaguppe, the country was free from hills but the soil was poorer.

Buchanan provided the following graphic description of the terrain of Turuvekere along with the ravages that were inflicted upon it, which is reflective of what large parts of the Mysore State had gone through in the decades gone by.

"**August 23. Appearance of the country**. - In the morning I was detained by a very heavy rain, which has given the people high spirits. In the afternoon I went two cosses to *Turiva-Caray,* the residence of the *Amildar.* The country afforded a melancholy prospect. Like that near *Bangalore,* and the other places towards the eastern *Ghats,* it rises into gentle swells, and occasionally projects a mass of naked granite, or of quartz blackened by iron; but it has once been completely cultivated; and every spot, except those covered by rock, bears marks of the plough. Scattered clumps of trees denote the former situations of numerous villages: all now, however, are nearly deserted. I saw only two houses; and a few fields ploughing for *Horse-gram* seemed to be the commencement of cultivation, from the time the country had been laid desolate by the merciless army of *Purseram Bhow.*"

From Turuvekere, Buchanan proceeded towards *Cada-hully* where the terrain was similar to that of *Arulu Gupay* and *Turiva-Caray*, but the soil was more inclined to be stony. Moving further, Buchanan went to *Belluru* where the greater part of the country consisted of barren heights covered with low bushes and had never been cultivated. As Buchanan travelled to Nagamangala the next day, he noticed that the terrain was similar to what he had seen the previous day with the exception that most of the areas, though barren, appeared as if they had been formerly cultivated. The country looked very bare with hardly any cultivation. Ruins of many villages were visible.

From Nagamangala, Buchanan went to a place called *Chinna*, which, according to Buchanan was more barren than that he had seen for some time; the heights rose to rocky hills. Some parts of the country were covered with low trees, especially with the *Elate sylvestris*, or wild date. *Chinna*, earlier a place of importance, was in ruins.

Buchanan's next destination was Melkote (*Mail-cotay*) where he stayed for two days (August 29-30, 1800). The terrain leading to Melkote was steep and nearly uninhabited. There were, however, many places on the ascent that had good soil, and that had been formerly cultivated. The other lands were covered with copse wood. Buchanan's last stop was at Tonnur (31st August, 1800). The intermediate country between Melkote and Tonnur was very rough, containing only a narrow fertile band on the sides of a water course, which, after heavy rain, used to carry the water from Melkote into the reservoir of Tonnur. The entire fertile band was formerly under cultivation which had diminished considerably, being limited to only a part of the band. Buchanan mentioned that there was an avenue plantation between Melkote and Tonnur to shelter the road and that the stumps of the avenue trees were still visible. Buchanan returned to Srirangapatna the next day (September 1, 1800).

It may be noted that throughout the entire stretch of his travel from Bangalore to Srirangapatna covering large parts of central Mysore and spanning about two months, Buchanan had not come across any area harboring good forest. Most of the vegetation met with consisted of low trees, copse wood or brushwood. As a matter of fact, Buchanan did not mention the names of any of the species that he had seen in these places except for a few such as *Elate sylvestris* which quite often colonized abandoned cultivations, or the *Chloroxylon Dupada* trees that had somehow survived atop a hill near Chikkanayakanahalli. We have indicated in an earlier chapter that Buchanan had mentioned about the presence of *Shorea talura* (jalari) trees in the hills of Madhugiri and its neighbourhood. The only patch of fairly good forest that Buchanan had come across during this leg of his journey was perhaps that of '*Bamboos*, and useless trees' in the Nandi hills. Here, the use of the phrase 'useless trees' by Buchanan may be viewed in the context that, perhaps the trees growing in the Nandi hills did not include teak or sandal and were therefore not considered as valuable or of any use. During those days, trees of other species, however luxuriant or well-grown they might have been, were not considered as useful. His comment that the fertile land of the Nandi hills might be brought into cultivation primarily echoed the mindset of people during those days that any land with good soil must be cleared for agriculture.

Natural vegetation on the south of Cavery

This leg of Buchanan's journey started from Srirangapatna on 5th September, 1800, and continued, as far as the Mysore territory was concerned, up to 3rd October, 1800, after which he entered the Company's territory (Madras Presidency) on his way to Malabar. However, as a part of the present Chamarajanagar district was then in the Company's territory, we will follow Buchanan for some distance (up to 10th October, 1800). During the period of over a month (5th September to 10th October, 1800), Buchanan visited a number of places in the present districts of Mandya (small portion), Mysuru and Chamarajanagar.

Buchanan's first halt was at Palahalli from where he proceeded to *Gungural-Chatur* located in the city district of Mysore. The country was uneven, but contained no hills. Much of the surface, especially towards the west, was broken, stony, and barren; but a great proportion had been formerly cultivated. From *Gungural-Chatur*, Buchanan proceeded further to Mullur (*Muluro*) via *Sicany-pura* or *Husein-pura*. At a short distance west from *Sicany-pura*, was the Lakshmana Tirtha River, originating in the hills of Coorg towards the south-west. The terrain through which Buchanan had travelled was no where steep and had a gentle upward slope. The area was covered with low trees. The growth of grass was better than common. As Buchanan proceeded towards the western *Ghats*, the luxuriance of the vegetation became more and more evident. After passing through places like *Emmaguma Cotagala* and *Katte Malalawadi*, Buchanan reached Periyapatna on 10ᵗʰ September, 1800. The region was hilly with tall trees which extended even to the summits of the hills. Although Periyapatna was located amidst rich vegetation, Buchanan had noticed deterioration in its natural environment due to human habitation and related activities. Buchanan's observations in this regard are significant in that these are relevant even today and are discernible in any landscape that is subjected to unplanned growth of human population without taking appropriate preventive measures.

> **"Environs of *Priya-pattana*.** – The environs of *Priya-pattana*, although rich and beautiful, are not at this season pleasant to a person living in tents; for the moisture of the climate, the softness of the soil, and the rankness of the vegetation, render every thing damp and disagreeable. Toward the east, the uncultivated grounds are half covered with dry thin bushes, especially the *Cassia auriculata*, and *Dodonea viscosa*; but here they are thickly clothed with herbage; and near the villages, where the ground is manured by the soil of the inhabitants, and of their cattle, the whole is covered with rank weeds, especially the *Ocymum molle*, Willd.? the *Datura metel*, the *Amaranthus spionosus*, the *Mirabilis jalappa*, and the *Tagetes erecta*; which last, although originally a native of *Peru*, is now naturalized every where, from *Hemada-giri* to *Rameswara*."

The richness of the forests of Periyapatna in terms of harboring sandalwood trees has already been mentioned in the *Chapter 2*. During his stay at Periyapatna Buchanan mentioned about the presence of elephants in these forests as follows:

> **"Elephants.** – The woods are infested by wild elephants, which do much injury to the crops. They are particularly destructive to the sugar-cane and palm-gardens; for these monstrous creatures break down the *Betel-nut* tree to get at its cabbage. The natives have

not the art of catching the elephant in *Kyaddas*, or folds, as is done in Bengal; but take them in pit-falls, by which a few only can be procured, and these are frequently injured by the fall."

After halting at Periyapatna for three days (September 11-13, 1800), Buchanan proceeded further towards *Hegodu Devana Cotay* (HD Kote) mainly with the intention of studying the surrounding forests. He camped in an abandoned village known as *Hejuru* located somewhere between Periyapatna and HD Kote. Buchanan provided the following account.

"Forests, September 16-18. – I remained at *Hejuru*, endeavouring to procure an account of the forests, in which I met with much less success than might reasonably have been expected. I went into them about three cosses, to a small tank, farther than which the natives rarely venture, and to which they do not go without being much alarmed on account of wild elephants. In this forest these animals are certainly more numerous, than either in *Chittagong* or *Pegu*. I have never seen any where so many traces of them. The natives, when they meet an elephant in the day-time, hide themselves in the grass, or behind bushes, and the animal does not search after them; but were he to see them, even at a distance, he would run at them, and put them to death. It is stragglers only from the herds, that in the day-time frequent the outer parts of the forest. The herds that at night destroy the crops, retire with the dawn of day into the recesses of the forest; and thither the natives do not venture, as they could not hide themselves from a number. It is said, that at the above-mentioned tank there was formerly a village; but that both it and several others on the skirt of the forest have been lately withdrawn, owing to an increased number of elephants, and to the smaller means of resistance which the decrease of population allows.

"Soil and appearance of the forests. – The soil of these forests is in general very good, and much of it is very black. In places where the water has lodged, and then dried up, such as in the print of an elephant's foot, this black soil assumes the appearance of indurated tar. The country is by no means steep, and is every where capable of cultivation; but of this no traces are to be seen in any part of the forest. Near *Hejuru* the trees are very small; for so soon as any one becomes of a useful size it is cut. As the distance and danger increase, the trees gradually are allowed to attain a larger growth; and at the tank they are of considerable dimensions. Farther on, they are said to be very stately. The forest is free from underwood or creepers; but the whole ground is covered with long grass, often as high as a man's head. This makes walking rather disagreeable and dangerous, as one is always liable to stumble over rotten trunks, to rouse a tiger, or to tread on a snake. These latter are said to be found of great dimensions, and have been seen as thick as the body of a middle-sized man. The length of this kind is not in proportion to the thickness, and does not exceed seven cubits. Although I passed a great part of these three days in the forest, I saw neither elephant, tiger, nor serpent, and escaped without any other injury than a fall over a rotten tree.

"Extent and produce of these forests. - These forests are very extensive, and reach to the foot of the western *Ghats*; but in this space there are many valuable and fertile tracts, belonging to the *Rajas* of *Coorg* and *Wynaad*. The trees on the *Ghats* are said to be the largest; yet in the dominions of *Mysore* there is much good timber. The kinds differ much less from those in the *Magadi* range of hills, than, considering the great difference of moisture and soil, might have been expected; for the rains here are copious, and the soil is rich; neither of which advantages are possessed by the central hills of the *Mysore Raja's* dominions. In the woods of *Hejuru*, however, there are very few of the prickly trees; whereas a large proportion of those at *Magadi* are *mimosas*.---"

In spite of the fact that Buchanan could get to see only a part of the forests around HD Kote, he examined forty (40) specimens of trees. On the basis of his observations of the trees and the specimens, and information elicited from the local people, Buchanan described the tree species along with their principal uses and other characteristics. The list of trees along with Buchanan's narration/comments has been appended at **Annexure II**.

From HD Kote Buchanan proceeded to Hampapura (September 20, 1800), where most of the areas had been cultivated in the past and out of these, about three fourths lay waste, having been abandoned by the cultivators. Buchanan also noticed that the soil had become drier than that met with earlier.

> "**Soil.** – We have now again got into a dry soil, with short herbage intermixed with bushes of the *Cassia auriculata*; but the fields have a verdure unknown to the eastward, and *Car' Ragy* is the common crop."

While travelling to *Maru-Hully* (Maruhalli) along a road parallel to the Kabini River, Buchanan had noticed a naturally beautiful valley with well-cultivated lands and harboring many trees, though few of them were large. The hills on the north and south were covered with bushes, so as to give them a uniform verdure in sync with the lush green valley. From Maruhalli Buchanan proceeded to Nanjangud along a road leading partly through among the small hills that bound the valley of the Kabini on the north, and partly through the valley itself. Among the hills, almost all the fields with good soil were under cultivation but many with poorer soil lay waste. Buchanan opined that the greater part of the area could never be made to produce anything but for some grass. From Nanjangud, Buchanan proceeded to Mysore through a country which had formerly been mostly cultivated but a large proportion of the fields had become waste, having been abandoned.

From Mysore, Buchanan travelled to Varakodu (*Waracadu*) through a terrain that had formerly been nearly all cultivated, and more than half of it was again occupied. Moving further, Buchanan travelled to a place called *Taiuru* by a road part of which passed among low hills covered with bushes, and abounding in antelopes. The soil of these hills was in general poor and full of small stones; but they were not occupied by naked rocks, like those on the north side of *Cavery*. From *Taiuru*, Buchanan travelled to Malinga (*Malingy*) via Narsipur. The mountainous tract which forms the western *Ghats* was visible from *Malingy*, and rose very high above the country to the westward.

From Malingy, Buchanan entered the Company's territory (October 3, 1800) and went to Kollegal and then to Sattegal. Buchanan mentioned about the presence of both sandal and teak trees in the forests of Kollegal; he found trees in these forests to be by and large stunted, good timber trees being available in some pockets of high forest such as *Mod-hully* and *Maha-deveswara*. Although sandalwood was found in the above-mentioned forests as well as in the skirts of the cultivated lands, the quality was not as good as that found in the western frontier.

After visiting the island of *Sivana Samudra*, and the waterfalls at *Gagana Chukki* and *Birra Chukki*, Buchanan proceeded to Hanur via *Singanaluru*. Near Hanur, he came across a hill known as *Hediny Betta*; it was the principal hill between the Cavery and the southern extremity of the eastern *Ghats* and harbored timber trees belonging to species such as teak, rosewood, honne, and jala.

Buchanan also mentioned about the prevalence of the system of shifting cultivation known as *Cotu-Cadu* in the forests of Kollegal (October 7, 1800).

> **"*Cotu-cadu* cultivation. –** In this hilly tract are a number of people, of a rude tribe called *Soligas*, or *Soligaru*, who use a kind of cultivation called the *Cotu-cadu*, which a good deal resembles that which in the eastern parts of Bengal is called *Jumea*. In the hot season the men cut the bushes that grow on any spot of land on the side or top of a mountain, where between the stones there is a tolerable soil. They burn the bushes when these have become dry, and leave to the women the remainder of the labour. When the rains commence, these with a small hoe dig up the ground to the depth of three inches. They then clear it of weeds, and next day sow it broad-cast with *Ragy*, here and there dropping in a seed of *Avaray*, *Tovaray*, mustard, maize, or pumpkin. The seed is covered by another hoeing. A woman in one day can hoe ten cubits square, and on the next can sow it. The sowing season lasts about two

months; so that the quantity sown in a year by every woman may be estimated at somewhat less than the sixth part of an acre. The custom however is, for all the people of one village to work one day at one family's ground, and the next day at another's at regular succession. The villages in general contain four or five families. The women perform also the whole harvest."

The *soligas* also raised plantain (banana) gardens by clearing the forest. Buchanan described the process of raising such gardens as follows:

"Plantain gardens, or those of the *Musa*. – These people have also plantain gardens. To form one of these, they cut down the bushes, and form pits with a sharp stick. In each of these they set a plantain-sucker, and ever afterwards keep down the grass and bushes, so as to prevent them from chocking the garden. The plantains are very large and coarse, and are eaten partly when ripe, and partly when green. Every family of the *Soligaru* pays annually to the government three *Fanams*, or about two shillings."

From Hanur, Buchanan proceeded (October 8, 1800) to Cowdalli through a hilly road that on the whole descended considerably. On the way, Buchanan noticed many small torrents that conveyed the rain water to the *Tati-hole*, a tributary of Cavery River. Next day, Buchanan travelled to *Mat-hully* or *Marat-hully* by a hilly road, steep in a few places, and surrounded by mountains. From *Mat-hully* (located near the border between present Karnataka and Tamil Nadu states), Buchanan continued his onward journey to Malabar via Coimbatore.

In this phase of his journey, Buchanan came across some excellent forests of the Mysore State in the Western *Ghats* region bordering the Coorg State. In the Kollegal region also, he came across extensive forests some of which harbored teak and sandalwood. However, by and large these forests were not as well-grown as the forests of the Western *Ghats*, and Buchanan generally referred to them as being of stunted to moderate growth.

Natural vegetation of the northern and central parts of Mysore State

After travelling through Malabar and Canara, Buchanan entered the Mysore State on 18th March, 1801 at Chandragutti in present Shivamogga district. During this phase of his journey in the northern and central parts of the Mysore State spanning more than two months (18th March to 3rd June, 1801), Buchanan visited a number of places in the present districts of Shivamogga, Davanagere, Chitradurga and Hassan.

Buchanan had found the terrain around Chandragutti to have been at one time almost entirely cultivated. A good part of this was overgrown with trees which had not yet arrived at their full height. Buchanan's mention about the presence of sandalwood trees in these forests has already been discussed in the *Chapter 2*. While going to Keladi (in Sagar taluk), he passed through a country greater part of which was pretty level; Buchanan opined that the higher grounds appeared to be entirely neglected; most of the trees were young and small; in places where they were large, they supported betel vines. Next day (March 21, 1801), he proceeded to Ikkeri through a country that was similar to what he had seen the previous day. Buchanan commented on the forests of the *Ghats* as follows:

> "**Forests of the Ghats**. – The *Sagar* district (*Taluc*) extends to the bottom of the mountains, on the declivity of which are many woods that spontaneously produce pepper. These forests are said to be very unhealthy." [Declivity means downward slope.]

Buchanan gave the following interesting account of the soil of the terrain after interacting with the local *Amildar*.

> "**Soil**. – The *Amildar*, who is a man of plain manners and good sense, says, that in this neighbourhood dry grains have been often tried, but have always failed; and that the goodness of the soil is merely apparent; for in general it is very shallow, and placed on a *substratum* of *Laterite*, which renders the soil above it very unproductive of grain. Even rice thrives ill, although the deepest and richest soils are reserved for its cultivation. It must

be observed, that in all the countries where it is found the opinion of the unfitness of the soil for dry grains is prevalent. The *Amildar* makes a curious observation. He says, that in the country to the eastward the surface is covered with stones; but under these there is a fine cool earth; while here, the surface is earth, but under that there is a dry rock which burns up every thing. It must, however, be observed, that the forests here are greatly superior to those farther east; owing probably, to the roots of trees being able to penetrate into the crevices of the rock, and to get at water, which is here generally found at no great depth from the surface: but to the eastward, before water can be procured, the wells must be dug to a considerable depth."

While narrating the appearance of the country on his way to a place called *Ghenasu-guli*, Buchanan made a few remarks which provide an insight to the formation of grassy blanks in high rainfall areas, a very common occurrence in the *malnad* region.

"**March 22. Appearance of the country**. – I went three cosses to *Ghenasu-guli*. The country all the way is hilly, and is considered by the natives as totally useless, although in many places the nature of the soil would admit of the use of the plough. It does not even answer for pasture, and the coarse, rank grass that grows upon it in the rainy season cannot be made into hay. Once a year, in order to keep the country clear, it is burned. This is probably the reason of the stunted appearance of the trees. On the whole, no desert in Africa can be less productive of use to man. ------"

It had been mentioned in a preceding chapter (*Chapter 6*) that in the forests of Canara, the practice of training naturally growing pepper vines upon trees was in vogue, and this resulted in very good production of black pepper which was an important commodity of trade. Having noticed that this practice was not prevalent in the pepper-vine bearing forests of the Mysore State, Buchanan made the following remarks.

"March 23. Wild pepper, and appearance of the country. – I went three cosses to *Duma*, or *Dumam*. The country resembles that which I came through yesterday, and on the whole way I did not see the smallest trace of cultivation. I passed through a very long wood where pepper grows spontaneously. The trees are very fine, and the soil is apparently good; but it is quite neglected by the natives, who say that the pepper is of no value. It is watered by the *Pada-gopi*, a rivulet that, after passing through the *Garsopa* district, falls into the inlet of the sea at *Honawera.---"*

On 25th March, 1801, Buchanan travelled to *Hyder Nagara* (now known as Nagara) through a fog so thick that he could see little of the country. It was extremely hilly and over grown with woods. After halting at *Hyder Nagara* for four days, Buchanan proceeded to *Cowldurga* (earlier known as *Bhavana-giri*) through a road which the whole way was exceedingly rough and hilly. The hills were covered with woods, most of which harbored the wild pepper vine; but these were quite neglected; and as they were not cultivated, although the village people collected a little pepper, they paid no rent. Buchanan opined that the absence of the stimulus of rent was the reason behind the neglect of these pepper growing forests by the local inhabitants.

From *Cowldurga*, Buchanan proceeded (March 30, 1801) to a place called *Hodalla* (perhaps Hodalakutra, near Thirthahalli town) passing through a village *Arga* (Araga), and then to another place called *Tuduru* (Tudur) on the next day (March 31, 1801). While there were thick forests near *Cowldurga*, the hills were tolerably well cleared towards *Hodalla*, and there were rice grounds in the intermediate little valleys. The greater part of the country near *Tuduru* was found to be covered with stunted woods. From *Tuduru*, Buchanan proceeded to *Baikshavani Mata* (April 1, 1801) and then to *Shiva-mogay* (Shimoga) on 2nd April, 1801. On the way, he passed through *Manday Gudday* (Mandagadde). In this stretch, along the bank of the Tunga River, Buchanan saw some excellent teak forests of the Mysore State. He also came across a forest having much sandalwood. These have already been discussed in some detail in *Chapter 3* and *Chapter 2*, respectively.

From Shimoga Buchanan proceeded to *Kudali*, the junction of the *Tunga* and *Bhadra* Rivers. He described the appearance of the country through which he had passed as follows:

> **"April 4. Appearance of the country.** – I went four cosses to *Kudali*. The country all the way is plain; but it contains many detached hills, some of which, toward the north, are pretty high. The whole country is bare, and almost entirely waste."

On the following day, Buchanan crossed the *Tungabhadra* River and proceeded to Sasvehalli (*Sahasiva-hully*). He noticed that the country on the west side of the river was in general level, but was interspersed with hills. The whole terrain was exceedingly bare. Buchanan's next destination was Basavapatna. He described the terrain through which he travelled to reach his destination in the following words.

> **"April 6. Appearance of the country.** – I went three cosses to *Baswa-pattana*, in order to avoid a steep mountainous road, called a *Ghat*, that lies in the direct route between *Sahasiva-hully*, and *Hari hara*. On the open country through which I passed, there are scattered several small hills. The soil in general seems to be capable of cultivation; but in other parts the rock comes to the surface, and much of it is waste. The farther I advanced into the open country, I observed that the villages are more strongly fortified. The country is very bare, and, like that to the eastward, is covered with bushes of the *Cassia auriculata*, and *Dodonaea viscosa*.

While travelling from Basavapatna to Malebennur (*Malaya Banuru*), Buchanan noticed that the low bare hills that formed the *Ghat* between *Sahasiva-hully* and *Hari hara* were visible on the left side of the road; all through the right side of the road was a fine level country, but it was exceedingly bare of trees. From Malebennur, Buchanan proceeded to Harihar through a plain country, with a few hills scattered at great distances. The country was exceedingly bare and arid.

After a halt of three days at Harihar, Buchanan proceeded to Davanagere (11th April, 1800). He noticed that, excepting three small hills near the road, the whole country was fit for cultivation. However, much of the land appeared to never have been cultivated, and was overgrown with bushes. Buchanan left Davanagere on 13th April and proceeded to Chitradurga via *Coduganur* and *Aligutta.* He passed through a barren country that was more or less plain, with low hills at a few places. From Chitradurga, he proceeded to Hiriyur via *Siddamana-hully* and *Imangala* (Aimangala). The road was mostly through a level country except for the stretch through the hills surrounding the plain of Chitradurga. The prolongation of the hills of Chitradurga was visible on the right side of the road. Greater part of the country was bare. Buchanan described the appearance of the country as he approached Hiriyur from Aimangala in the following words.

> "**April 19. Appearance of the country**. – I went three cosses to *Heriuru*, near which a great change takes place in the appearance of the country. The soil is mostly stony, and at this season exceedingly parched; so that there is scarcely any grass, and the only green things to be seen are a few scattered *Mimosas.*"

After prolonged stay at Hiriyur necessitated by the illness of some of his accompanying staff, Buchanan resumed his journey on May 2, 1801. On his way to Yelladakere (*Ellady-caray*), he described the appearance of the surrounding country in the following words.

> "**May 2. Appearance of the country**. In the morning I went four cosses to *Ellady-caray*, which is situated among the low hills running S. E. from *Chatrakal.* I saw no houses by the way; but some must have been near my route, as in different places I observed a few fields that were cultivated. I passed through several ruined villages. The appearance of the country is desolate, and it is said never to have been much better, in the memory of man. The soil is entirely poor stony land; and the naked rocks, in a state of decay, come frequently to the surface. The grass in many places is long, but at this season it is quite withered; and the only things green, that are visible, are a few wild date palms (*Elate sylvestris*), most of which are young. In moist places they grow spontaneously, and produce juice, which is often boiled into *Jagory.* The hills are of no

considerable height, and among them there is much plain ground. By the natives this is considered as of very little use; but to me, much of it appears to be very capable of being rendered productive, whenever labourers and stock can be found."

As Buchanan travelled further and crossed a hilly terrain, he came across forests covered with trees: 'On the hills, there are a good many stunted trees.'

After inspecting a number of iron ore mines in the region, and studying about glass-making works at a place called Mathodu (*Muteodo*), Buchanan proceeded to Hosadurga through a country that was not hilly and was fit for cultivation; but almost the whole area lay waste, cultivation being very limited. Towards the east was a range of hills running from *Chatrakal* to *Chica Nayakana hully*. Towards the west was a level country, interspersed with a few detached hills. From Hosadurga, Buchanan proceeded further towards *Banawara* via a number of places such as *Belluguru, Budihalu*, and *Garuda-giri*. The surrounding land was level, with stony or gravelly soil but fit enough for cultivation. Some of these areas had suffered a lot of depredations during the Maratha invasions. The *Garuda-giri* hill had some sandal and *lac* trees. Buchanan had noticed that the *Elate sylvestris* or wild date trees were very common in the wastelands including abandoned cultivations. In and around Javagal (*Jamagallu*), which Buchanan visited next, the wild date had overgrown most of the areas which once were rice fields.

On 12th May, Buchanan proceeded from Javagal (*Jamagallu*) to Halebeedu (*Hulleybedu*) through a country that had good soil but was quite deserted; by the way he observed some small hills consisting entirely of calcareous tufa, mixed with a little earth. His next destination was Belur (*Bailuru*). The road to *Bailuru* passed through a bare country part of which was hilly and full of stones. Buchanan mentioned about having crossed a river named *Bhadri* near *Bailuru*. Apparently, *Bhadri* was the old name of the river which now is known as Yagachi. Buchanan also mentioned that to the west of the *Bhadri* river the country was called *Malayar*, or the hills; while that on the eastern side was called *Meidan*, or the open country. Buchanan gave the following description of the *Malayar* country.

"**Country called *Malayar*.** - The nature of the *Malayar* country resembles that of the sea coast below the western *Ghats*, in so far as rice is the principal object of cultivation, and as little attention is paid to the rearing of dry grains upon which the people to the north and west of *Bhadri* chiefly subsist. In the *Malayar* country, however, there are no pepper gardens, nor plantations of *betel-nut* palms, for which it seems as well fitted as the *Nagara* principality. It is said entirely to resemble the *Codagu Rayada*, or *Coorg* country. At *Bailuru* there is no brickstone, and the country abounds with the calcareous *tufa*. The hills are overgrown with wood, and are considered as quite useless. The vallies only are cultivated."

From *Bailuru* (Belur) Buchanan proceeded to a place called *Haltoray* through a country that was very bare. Next day he proceeded to Hassan (*Hasina*) through a country that was fine *Ragy* land, but very little of it was cultivated. From Hassan Buchanan went to a place called *Grama* where the soil was abundantly good, growing both rice and *Ragy*. Thereafter, he went to Channarayapatna (*Chin-raya-patna*) where the country was naturally pretty but was exceedingly bare, having hardly either trees or fences. Buchanan's next destination was *Sravana Belgula* (19th May, 1801). The route was through a country which according to Buchanan appeared to be almost entirely waste. Due to severe eye ailment, Buchanan was not in a position to complete his inspections of *Sravana Belgula* to the extent that he would have wished. He therefore proceeded to Srirangapatna for recuperation.

In this phase of his journey Buchanan came across some of the best forests of the Mysore State such as the teak forests of Shimoga on the bank of the Tunga River. He had also passed through some excellent evergreen forests near *Nagara, Cowldurga, Sagara*, etc. Buchanan had referred to these forests as natural pepper-vine-bearing forests. These forests are primarily located in the western part of the present Shivamogga district. As regards the natural vegetation of the remaining districts such as Chitradurga, Davanagere and Hassan, it was by and large similar to that of the districts such as Tumkur, Kolar, etc.

Natural vegetation from Srirangapatna to Malalawadi

The last leg of Buchanan's journey in the Mysore State, which was also his return journey to Madras, started on 4th June, 1801. He went to a place called *Banuru*, initially passing through irrigated rice grounds, bounded toward the north by low hills, and then through a widened level country that was mostly arable, but little of it under irrigation. Buchanan noticed that many of the farmlands were interspersed with *Mimosa indica* trees (present name *Acacia nilotica* – karijali/babul). Next day, he proceeded to a place called *Sosila* (Sosale) through a plain country interspersed with a few small hills. In some places the soil was very sandy. The area was neither so well-wooded nor so well-enclosed as he had seen the previous day. His next place of halt was *Kirigavil* which he reached by passing through a country comprising mostly dry arable land but much of it was waste. He had also crossed one small ridge of hills, consisting of naked rocks of white granite.

On 8th June, 1801, Buchanan went to *Malawully* (Malavalli) through a country that looked capable of cultivation; indeed there were signs indicating that the entire area once was under the plough and was enclosed with quickest hedges. Next day, Buchanan went to a place called *Hulluguru*. For the first half of the way the country resembled that through which he had come the previous day. Afterwards it became poorer and poorer, and was covered with low *Mimosas*. Buchanan mentioned about the presence of two hills in the neighbourhood of *Hulluguru*, namely, *Basawana-Betta* and *Capala-durga*, which had some sandalwood trees and abundant bamboos but did not have any valuable timber trees. On 10th June, Buchanan went to *Sathnur* through a pretty wide valley, with hills on both sides of the road. The soil in general was poor, and much of it was over-run with low *Mimosas* and other bushes. Next day, he went to *Canicarna-hully*, commonly called *Cancan-hully* (present Kanakapura). The road by which Buchanan travelled passed through a valley, in some places narrow and rocky, and in others wide, partly cultivated, and partly overgrown with low trees. The hills surrounding the valley were very rocky, and were said to be much infested by tigers.

After halting at *Cancan-hully* (Kanakapura) for a couple of days, Buchanan proceeded to *Malalawady* (Malalawadi) on 13th June, 1801. The greater part of the country through which he passed was overgrown with low trees and bushes, and very little of what was arable was actually cultivated. *Malalawady* was the last place of Buchanan's visit in the Mysore State. On 14th June, 1801, he left *Malalawady* for *Tully*, situated in the Company's territory, on way to Madras.

The last leg of Buchanan's journey in the Mysore State spanning ten days covered parts of the present districts of Mysuru, Mandya and Ramanagara. A considerable part of the road was through relatively hilly terrain harboring low trees and bushes. Although the landscape did not harbor tall trees, it appeared to have been fairly well-clothed with trees of low to medium growth belonging to species typical of dry deciduous and scrub forests with preponderance of thorny *Acacias.*

AN OVERVIEW OF THE FORESTS OF MYSORE STATE

From what has been narrated above, it is evident that Buchanan had travelled quite extensively throughout the length and breadth of the Mysore State. He had covered substantial areas coming under all but one districts of the present Karnataka State which then were included in the princely state of Mysore, the lone exception being the Chikkamagaluru district. However, the *Malayar* country lying on the west of the *Bhadri* (Yagachi) river, which Buchanan had referred to when passing through Belur (*Bailur*), included a portion of the present Chikkamagaluru district also, besides a portion of Hassan district. Buchanan had also visited the Kollegal region, which then was administered directly by the East India Company and which now is a part of the Chamarajanagar district.

Although Buchanan had travelled through a number of forest areas of Mysore State, he had provided details of the tree species occurring in the forests on two occasions. During his visit to the Savana-durga forests in Magadi, he provided details of seventy (70) tree species (**Annexure-I**). During his tour through the forests of HD Kote on the foothills of the Western *Ghats*, he had identified forty (40) tree species (**Annexure-II**). In respect of the forests of HD Kote, Buchanan had admitted that the number of tree species identified was less as he could visit only a part of the forest. Perusal of Annexure-I and Annexure-II brings out a few significant facts: Both the lists primarily contain tree species that are typical of deciduous forests; teak is present in both. Most of the species included in Annexure-II

(HD Kote forests) are included in Annexure-I (Savana-durga forests) also. However, the trees at Annexure-II have been described as larger than the trees at Annexure-I. In the forests of Savana-durga, two species of bamboo were present, one hollow and another solid. However, only one species (hollow) was present in the HD Kote forests. The hollow and solid bamboo species were presumably *Bambusa bambos* (dowga) and *Dendrocalamus strictus* (medri), respectively. Another fact, which was also pointed out by Buchanan, was that the Savana-durga forests had more thorny species than the HD Kote forests; this is indicative of the fact that the Savana-durga forests were situated on relatively drier tract than the HD Kote forests which were favored by copious rains of the Western *Ghats*.

The above characteristics broadly indicate that the HD Kote forests belonged to the type 'Teak-bearing moist deciduous forest', whereas the Savana-durga forests belonged to the type 'Teak-bearing dry deciduous forest' with patches of scrub forest in drier sites. It must also be added that the Savana-durga forest, with a fairly wide diversity of species, perhaps represented one of the best dry deciduous forests of the Mysore State. As a matter of fact, the presence of *Chukrasia tabularis* in Annexure-I provides a hint of moist deciduous vegetation in pockets of Savana-durga forests. Such occurrence is generally noticed in valleys and depressions of well-protected dry deciduous forests.

As we have mentioned in *Chapter 3*, Buchanan had come across an excellent forest containing teak and bamboo on the bank of the Tunga River near Shimoga. He was so much impressed with the growth of teak in the forest that he expressed the opinion that all the less valuable trees from the forest should be replaced by taking up teak planting. Buchanan did not provide details of the other species present in the forest. However, considering the excellent growth of teak as expressed by Buchanan and also the fact that teak always comes up in association of bamboo and a number of hardwood species such as the *Terminalias, Dalbergia latifolia, Pterocarpus marsupium, Lagerstroemia lanceolata, Adina cordifolia*, etc., it can be inferred that the teak forest at Shimoga seen by Buchanan was a 'teak-bearing moist deciduous forest.'

Buchanan mentioned about the presence of pepper-vine bearing forests in Nagara, Sagara, Kaval durga, etc. These are primarily tropical wet evergreen forests. These forests mainly harbor softwood trees along with some medium-hardwood and a few hardwood trees. However, due to availability of large quantities of hardwood timber in the deciduous forests, the trees of the evergreen forests were considered useless for a long time in the past, and it was thought prudent to sacrifice such forests in favour of encouraging naturally growing pepper-vines to boost production of black pepper which was an important spice for local consumption besides trade and export. Buchanan also hinted at the presence of useless forest in the *Malayar* country lying on the west side of the *Bhadri* (Yagachi) river. Parts of present Hassan and Chikkamagaluru districts can be said to fall in the *Malayar* country. These forests were also primarily evergreen forests that were considered useless for a long time.

In addition to the above, Buchanan's narrations also indicate the presence of noticeable forest (with or without teak/sandalwood) at a few places such as Kollegal, Channapatna, Malavalli, Kanakapura (*Cancanhully*), Sathnur, Nandi hills, Basavanabetta, etc. Keeping these in view, the overall forest scenario of Mysore State at the beginning of the nineteenth century may be depicted as follows:

The present districts of Mysuru, Chamarajanagar, Ramanagara, Shivamogga, Chikkamagaluru (part), Hassan (part), Chikkaballapur (part), and Mandya (part) had moderate to very good forests. The remaining districts, more notably, Kolar, Chitradurga, Davanagere, Tumkur, Bangalore Urban, Bangalore Rural, Hassan (part), etc. had harbored forests of poor quality comprising low or stunted dry deciduous and scrub forests. It may, however, be mentioned that even in these districts there were some good forest patches of *Shorea talura, Elate sylvestris*, etc. In fact, Madhugiri areas of Tumkur district were the main source of *Lac* during those days. Bangalore and Chikkaballapur areas were also particularly known for forests harboring *Shorea talura* trees.

It may also be pointed out that the route along which Buchanan had travelled in the Mysore State was largely flanked by habitations and agricultural fields (including abandoned cultivations). Besides, he had visited most of the areas of the State where mining and smelting of iron ore were in progress. As already mentioned, large quantities of charcoal were required for running the forges/furnaces for the production of iron and steel. This had invariably put a lot of pressure on the surrounding vegetation resulting in its near decimation. Therefore, Buchanan's impressions about the natural vegetation of the surrounding country were based largely on what he had seen on both sides of the road that he travelled by. Under such circumstances, it was humanly impossible for anyone to make an assessment of the natural vegetation of the entire terrain, especially in respect of the areas located far away from the road. This is more relevant in case of forest vegetation, because, more often than not, better forests are located farther from habitations.

During the course of his journey Buchanan had come to know about the presence of tiger and its menace in a number of places that he had passed through. The animal was reported not only from areas harboring good forest but also from areas which Buchanan had assessed to be of poor quality in terms of natural vegetation. By and large, presence of tiger in any location is indicative of the existence of reasonably good forest in the vicinity. It will therefore be of some interest to enumerate the places in the Mysore State which as per Buchanan's narrations were frequented by tigers.

Presence of Tiger in Mysore State

During his travel through Mysore State, Buchanan was informed about the presence of tiger and depredations caused by the animal in the following places:

1. *Rama-giri* ['The place is dreadfully infested by tigers, especially the fort, which occupies a large rocky hill, ---' Page 163, Vol. I.] Also at Bidadi or Wiridy ['Tigers are very numerous among the copse;' Page 49, Vol. I.]

2. *Madhugiri* [Killing or wounding of cattle belonging to the *Goalas* by tigers. Page 11-12, Vol. II.]

3. *Cada-hully*, situated between Turuvekere and Belluru [Tigers preyed upon the sheep belonging to the shepherds. Page 61; Vol. II.]

4. *Periyapatna* [Tigers in the ruins of the fort. Page 96, Vol. II.]

5. *Hanagodu* and the neighbouring country [The country is infested with tigers and elephants that are very destructive. Page 118, Vol. II.]

6. *Heggadadevanacotay* [The *Curubaru* frequently suffer from tigers. Page 127, Vol. II.]

7. *Gagana Chukki* [Tigers in the Mussulman hermitage. Page 168, Vol. II.]

8. *Sahasiva-hully* [Tigers more destructive here than in the woods. Page 304, Vol. III.]

9. *Chica-bayli-caray* [Mining and smelting works affected due to killing of people by tigers in *Chica-bayli-caray*, *Buca Sagurada Canavay* and *Cudure Canavay*. Page 361, Vol. III.]

10. *Muteodu* [Villages including *Lacky hully* were infested by tigers. Page 367, Vol. III.]

11. *Garuda-giri* [Lac collection was given up owing to increasing number of tigers. Page 383, Vol. III.]

12. *Cancan-hully* [The surrounding hills were said to be much infested by tigers. Page 425, Vol. III.]

13. *Cancan-hully* [During the last two years of the Sultan's government, eighty inhabitants of *Cancan-hully* were carried away by tigers from within the walls of the fort. Page 427, Vol. III.]

The presence of tiger in places such as Periyapatna, Bidadi, *Hanagodu, Heggadadevanacotay, Rama-giri, Gagana Chukki* and *Cancan-hully* was quite understandable, given that these areas as per Buchanan's observations had moderate to excellent forest. However, the presence of tiger in places such as *Madhugiri, Cada-hully, Sahasiva-hully, Chica-bayli-caray, Buca Sagurada Canavay, Cudure Canavay, Muteodu*, and *Garuda-giri* is indicative of the fact that these places also had in their vicinity some forest areas of sufficient growth and cover to afford protection to an animal like tiger, although these forests might have been situated away from the route that Buchanan had travelled by. These places are located in the present districts of Tumkur, Davanagere, Chitradurga and Hassan (eastern part) which represented the dryer parts of the Mysore State.

Presence of Leopard in the Mysore State

Interestingly, during his entire travel through Mysore and Canara, Buchanan came to know about the presence of the animal leopard (panther) only on one occasion: On April 13, 1801, during his halt at a place called *Coduganur* (between Davanagere and Chitradurga), a leopard that had earlier killed several oxen and attacked a number of men was killed by the people of the village and brought to his tent. Generally, a leopard is at home both in high forest and in scrub forest. The fact that the menace of leopard was quite rare during those days is indicative of the richness of the vegetation that occurred in the vicinity of habitations. Unlike the scrub forests of today which do not harbor any smaller animal for the leopard to prey upon, even the relatively degraded forests that had occurred in the past around human habitations must have harbored sufficient numbers of smaller animals and as a result, the leopards hardly had any need or compulsion to come out and hunt for cattle, dogs, and even human beings in the villages and towns, as they quite often do nowadays.

Presence of an interesting animal in Savanadurga forests

During his tour through the forests of Savanadurga, Buchanan was informed of an interesting dog-like animal that inhabited these forests. Buchanan described as follows (20th June, 1800):

> **"Two wild animals of the dog kind**. – It is said, that in the great forests round *Savana-durga*, there is a small animal called the *Shin-Nai*, or red dog, which fastens itself by surprise on the neck of the tiger, and kills him. On this account the tiger is not so common in these large forests, as in the smaller woods. The *Shin-Nai* is quite distinct from the wild dog, which is said to be very common here, to grow to a large size, and to be very destructive to sheep. By this wild dog the natives probably mean the wolf. I have seen native drawings of the *Shin-Nai*, which appear to represent an animal not yet described."

It is likely that the red dog (*Shin-Nai*) that Buchanan was informed about as being present in the Savanadurga forests could have been the

Dhole or the Indian wild dog (*Cuon alpinus*), which is also known as red dog. Although this animal individually is no match for the tiger, large packs of wild dogs are capable of confronting and sometimes injuring the tiger. We have seen that during the time when Buchanan had visited the Mysore State, the Savanadurga forests were fairly rich and dense; such forests then must have been capable of harboring the wild dog, which now is found only in the dense forests of the Western *Ghats* region. The other dog-like animal, as Buchanan had guessed, was perhaps the Indian wolf (*Canis lupus pallipes*), which is quite common in the dry deciduous forests of Karnataka.

FOREST MANAGEMENT

As mentioned earlier, the concept of forest as an administrative unit had not evolved during the time when Buchanan had visited Mysore. However, government and the people were aware of the importance of many trees growing in the forest, as certain goods required by the people were sourced from these trees. Therefore, these trees became an important source of revenue for the government; collection and processing of the forest produces became an important avenue of employment for certain sections or communities of the people. In view of these direct benefits accruing from the trees, gradually a system of husbanding or conserving the trees evolved, which eventually led to development of the concept of forest management.

In his travel-diaries Buchanan had mentioned a number of times about an official who was in charge of protection of trees. During his halt at Madhugiri (July 25-29, 1800), he provided the following description of an official called *Gydda Cavila*.

> **"Gydda Cavila, or keeper of forests**. – In every *Taluc*, or district, where there are forests, there is a *Gydda Cavila*, who annually pays to the government a certain sum, and has the exclusive privilege of collecting honey, wax, and lac. On all such as cut timber for building their houses, he also levies a duty; and all the trees, except sandal-wood, are in fact his property. The government ought to pay him for all the trees which it requires; but this is generally omitted,

an Indian government rarely paying for anything which it can get by force. The keeper of the forest exacts also small duties on those who, without being privileged, feed their goats and cattle in the woods; on the women, who collect the leaves, which are used as platters by all ranks in this country; and on those who collect firewood, and grass for thatch."

Buchanan also mentioned about the post of an official known as *Gyda Cavila* which had formerly existed in the forests of Periyapatna. He described as follows:

"**September 11-13. Forests**. - There is at present no *Gyda Cavila*, or forest-renter; but formerly there used to be one, who, having made friendship with the wild tribes called *Cad' Eravaru*, and *Jain Curubaru*, procured from them honey and wax, *Popli chica*, a dye, *Dupada* wood, *Gunti Beru*, a root used in dyeing, *Cad' Arsina*, or wild turmeric, and *Cadu Baly Aly*, or the leaves of the wild plantain tree, which are used by the natives as dishes. For timber, or grass, no rent was demanded."

There was also a system of renting out certain trees in an area to an individual for certain sum of money. This individual would further sub-let the trees to various people. We had seen this system in respect of the wild date or *Elate sylvestris* trees at Madhugiri.

During his travel through *Singanaluru* in the Kollegal region (October 6, 1800), Buchanan had mentioned that the *Gydda Cavila*, or forest renter, was not there.

In the absence of special government official to collect the rent of forest produce, the village *Gaudas* used to don the role of the keeper of forest and permit certain groups of people to collect forest products including dyes, drugs, medicines, etc. on payment of rent.

Chapter 10

FORESTS OF CANARA

After touring Malabar, Buchanan entered Canara on the 15th of January, 1801. Till 22nd January, Buchanan travelled through that part of Canara which now falls in the Kasaragod district of Kerala State. He arrived at *Ulala* (Ullal, situated south of Mangalore) on 22nd January, 1801, and this day may be reckoned as the date of Buchanan's entry to what represents the present Karnataka State.

After staying at Mangalore for seven days, Buchanan proceeded to *Arcola*, also known as *Feringy-petta,* on 29th January, 1801. He found that the whole country entirely resembled Malabar except that in this part of Canara, terraces were formed at the roots of the hills only, unlike in the Malabar where steep sides of the hills were formed into terraces. Buchanan was told by the local people that less than one fourth of the ground fit for garden was actually planted. He was also told that '*Tippoo*, in order to remove every inducement for Europeans to frequent the country, destroyed all the pepper vines, and all the trees on which these were supported'.

On 31st January, 1801, Buchanan proceeded to *Nagara Agrarum*, passing through a town named *Buntwala.* He found the country similar to that between Mangalore and *Arcola*. Most of the hills were clear; but many palms of the *Borassus* kind were scattered throughout the country, and the little vallies were finely watered with clear perennial rivulets. Next day, Buchanan went to a place called *Cavila-cutty*. Buchanan described the appearance of the country as follows:

"**February 1. Appearance of the country**. – I went three cosses to *Cavila-cutty*. The hills are much higher than those to the westward, and some of them are covered with tall thick forests, in which are found *Teak* (*Theka*) and wild *Mango* (*Mangifera*) trees, and the palm which Linnaeus called *Caryota*. These hills abound with tigers, which have of late killed several passengers. The road all the way is tolerably well formed, but the engineer has paid no attention to avoid hills: some parts of it are excessively steep. I passed many oxen, loaded with salt, going to the *Mysore* dominions, and met many coming from thence loaded with iron."

On 2ⁿᵈ February, Buchanan went to a place called *Bellata Angady* (Belthangady). While narrating the appearance of the country, he mentioned about the nearby hills in the following words.

"---On the hills many trees have now grown up; but it would appear, that formerly they had been all cleared; and to keep the bushes down, and to destroy vermin, the grass is still annually burned.---"

Next day, Buchanan proceeded to a place called *Jamal-abad*. He described the appearance of the country through which he had travelled as follows:

"**February 3. Appearance of the country**. - I went a short journey to *Jamal-abad*, which originally was called *Narasingha Angady*. The country through which I passed to-day is almost entirely covered with wood; but much of it has a good soil, and might be watered by means of the small river which we twice crossed. The road is very good."

In the vicinity of *Jamal-abad*, Buchanan had noticed the prevalence of the practice of shifting cultivation in forest areas. He gave the following description of the practice, locally called *Cotucadu* or *Cumri*, and its effect on the forest vegetation.

"*Malayar*, and their manner of cultivating the hills. - In this neighbourhood, the hills that are cultivated after the *Cotucadu* or *Cumri* manner are all private property. The *Mulucaras*, or proprietors, have alienated the whole right of cultivating them to a rude tribe, called *Malayar*, or *Malay-cudies*. The *Malayar*, who dwells on any hill of this kind has the exclusive hereditary right of cultivating it; but, while not occupied by this labour, he and his family must work for the proprietor (*Mulucara*), at the allowance of provisions usually given to slaves. The *Malayar* may give up his possession when he pleases, which secures him from being ill used by the proprietor; for such people on an estate add greatly to its value. They work for their master ten months in the year; but, having six or seven miles to come and go from their hills to their master's fields, they labour only six hours in the day. In this neighbourhood no tax is imposed on this kind of land; but in some districts the *Malayar* pay annually a small sum to government for each hill.

"The following is the manner in which this sort of cultivation, called *Cumri*, is performed. In the beginning of the dry season, the *Malayar* cuts down all the trees and bushes from a certain space of ground, and before the rains set in he burns them. The ground is then dug with a sharp *Bamboo*, and sown with *Shamay* (*Panicum miliare*), *Ragy* (*Cynosurus Corocanus*), rice, and various cucurbitaceous plants. The grains are sown separately; but seeds of the cucurbitaceous fruits are mixed with all the farinaceous crops. With the *Ragy* are also mixed the seed of *Hibary* (*Cytisus Cajan*), and of *Abary* (*Dolichos Lablab*). Next year another piece of ground must be cleared, the former not being fit for cultivation in less than twelve years. In *Tulava*, this is the only kind of cultivation of dry grains, although much of the ground seems fit for the purpose; but the natives have a notion, that no high ground can produce any thing unless a great deal of timber has been burned on it.

"Hills of *Tulava* considered as useless. Hay. – They therefore consider the greater part of the country as totally useless, except for pasture or hay, and very little of it produces the proper grass. One kind of grass only that is produced in *Tulava* is eatable; and when I proposed to the natives to destroy the bad kinds, and sow the seed of the good, they were filled with astonishment at what they considered as the extravagance of the project. Where the hills are not too steep for the plough, I am persuaded that this might be done to great advantage; and the quantity of live stock and manure might be thus quadrupled. The hay at present is very bad, and sapless; for the grass, in its natural state, withers from maturity, before the rainy season is over; and before that period the hay could not be preserved. This, however, might be easily remedied, by cutting the grass while young, and allowing a second crop to come up, so as to be in juice at the commencement of the fair weather. The first crop would make good manure. This project the natives consider as equally extravagant with the former; nor indeed can it be expected, that in their circumstances they should attempt any innovation of the kind, until convinced, by an experiment made before their eyes, that it would succeed."

[**Note:** *Tulava* refers to that portion of *Canara* where *Tulu* was the principal language spoken by the people. The northern limit of the *Tulava* country extended to the south of Bhatkal, i.e. up to Baindur.]

On 4th February, Buchanan returned to *Bellata-Angadi* by the same road and then turned toward north to a place called *Padanguddy* by a good road through a country that was clear; the hills were low and of gentle downward slope. Next day, he proceeded towards *Sopina Angady*. From *Padanguddy* to the banks of the northern branch of the *Mangalore* river at *Einuru*, the country was much like what he had seen the previous day, but more woody. Between the river and *Sopina Angady*, the hills were steeper, and consequently the road was very bad. Buchanan mentioned about the menace of tigers in *Sopina Angady* and also described how its inhabitants got rid of the animals.

"**February 5. Tigers**. -----The place was formerly much infested with tigers; but a year ago the inhabitants collected, and cleared away so much of the wood, that they now have no trouble from these animals. They clear the country by cutting down the brush-wood, and burning it when it has dried. If this be repeated two or three years successively, the large trees also decay. The country is afterwards preserved clear by annually burning the grass. A few bushes always spring up, but not more than is sufficient to supply the farmers with leaves for manure."

Buchanan described the appearance of the country as he proceeded to his next destination Moodabidri as follows:

"**February 6. Appearance of the country**. - I went two cosses to *Mudu*, or East *Biddery*, and by the way crossed a branch of the northern *Mangalore* river, which descends from the *Ghats*. On the way, two tigers were seen by some of my people. Although the country is well cleared, it contains very little rice ground; and, as the hills are considered as totally useless, this is in fact one of the poorest countries that I have ever seen."

On 7th February, 1801, Buchanan travelled to *Carculla* (Karkala). The first part of the road was through a tolerably level country. Near *Carculla* the hills were steep and rocky, and some of them were overgrown with trees. After halting at *Carculla* for two days, Buchanan went to a place called *Beiluru* through a rather woody country where granite rocks were quite conspicuous on the high lands. Next day, Buchanan went to a place called *Haryadika*. Here, Buchanan had interaction with the local people regarding the possibility of taking up cultivation on the hills.

"**Feb. 10. Hills capable of cultivation**. - I went three cosses to *Haryadika*. The country is similar to that through which I came yesterday. The farmers here say, that all the hills, wherever the soil is free from rock, might be converted into *Betta-land*. The quantity of such grounds, they say, is very considerable; at least three times as much as is cultivated; but, they add, the expense is great, and the returns are small. About a fourth part of what was formerly cultivated is now waste, for want of people and stock.

Until that be fully occupied, no experiments on new land would be proper. The people say, that they would be willing to bring this new land into cultivation on the following conditions. The whole expense attending the various operations being collected into a sum, they should pay no revenue to the government until that was reimbursed by the usual amount of the land-tax, which is from one to three *Sultany Fanams* for a *Moray* sowing, or from rather more than 6½*d.* to almost 1*s.* 11*d.* an acre."

On 11th February, Buchanan went to Udupi through a country that was similar to that he passed through on the two preceding days. Near Udupi, the strata of granite, however, were mostly covered by the *Laterite*.

On 12th February, 1801, Buchanan went to *Brahma-wara* through a country of gently rising hills, free of woods, but the road was finely sheltered by avenue trees of *Vateria indica*, or the *Dupada Maram*. Next day, he went to a place called *Hirtitty* by a road most part of which passed along a low sandy ridge; on either side of the ridge were extensive rice grounds. The country looked well; for even the greater part of the sandy ridge was fenced, and planted for timber and fuel wood trees. There was a river called *Mabucullu* which descended from the *Ghats*. The banks of the river were well planted with coco-nut trees.

On 14th February, 1801, Buchanan went to *Kundapur*. The country between *Hirtitty* and *Kundapur* was similar to that between *Brahma-wara* and *Hirtitty*, except that there was by the way neither river nor coco-nut plantations; the extent of rice ground was smaller. After halting at *Kundapur* for two days, he went to *Beiduru* (Baindur) on 17th February. On the way there was much rice ground, and the crops looked well.

When travelling to *Batuculla* (Bhatkal), Buchanan described the terrain from *Beiduru* to *Batuculla* as follows:

"February 18th. – I went four cosses to *Batuculla*, which means the *round town*. A very steep barren ridge separates *Beiduru* from a fine level, which is watered by the *Combara*, a small slow running stream, that in several places is dammed up for the irrigation of the fields. Here was formerly a market (*Bazar*) named *Hosso-petta*, which General Mathews destroyed. After passing this level, I came to a very barren country, but not remarkably hilly. It is covered with stunted trees, and intersected by a small rapid stream, the *Sancada-gonda*, and farther on by a narrow cultivated valley. *Batuculla* stands on the north bank of a small river, the *Sancada-holay*, which waters a very beautiful valley surrounded on every side by hills, and in an excellent state of cultivation. ----"

On 19th February, Buchanan went to a place called *Shiraly*. The country, after ascending the little hill above *Batuculla* was not steep, but much of the soil was very poor, in many places the *Laterite* being almost entirely naked. In some other places the soil was very good, and, although not level, a part of it had been formed into *Betta* land for the cultivation of rice. This, Buchanan opined, 'confirms the account given by the people of *Haryadika*, concerning the possibility of rendering all the hills of *Canara* arable. In general, however, they are considered as not fit for this purpose'.

From *Shiraly*, Buchanan went to a place called *Beiluru* through a plain between the sea and the low hills; the breadth of the plain varied from half a mile to a mile and a half. On 21st February, he travelled to a place called *Cassergoda* which was situated on the south side of the *Honawera* lake. The country from *Beiluru* to *Cassergoda* was very barren consisting of low hills of *Laterite* which extended down to the sea, and were almost devoid of soil. In some places a few stunted trees were visible; but in general the rock was thinly scattered with tufts of grass, or of thorny plants.

On February 22, 1801, after crossing the inlet or lake at *Honawera*, Buchanan went to *Hulledy-pura* (Haldipur), where the *Tahsildar* of *Honawera* resided. He halted at *Hulledy-pura* for two days. During this period Buchanan acquainted himself with various aspects such as land tenure, agricultural practices, commerce, currencies, weights and measures, etc. of the *Haiga* country. [**Note:** *Haiga* country refers to the region of *Canara* primarily occupied by the community known as *Havika*. It starts from Bhatkal and continues up to Gokarna, and includes the portion of Canara above the *Ghats* such as Sirsi, Sonda, Bilgi, etc. The northern part of Canara beyond Gokarna has been referred to as *Kankana* and includes Ankola, Sadashivagad, etc.]

During his stay at *Hulledy-pura,* Buchanan learnt about the practice of cultivation in *Betta,* or hill land which he described as follows:

> "**Betta, or hill land**. – The land called here *Betta,* or *Hackelu,* like the *Parum* of *Malabar,* is formed into terraces; but on these rice is not cultivated. The only crops that it produces are *Sesamum* and *Udu* (*Phaseolus minimoo* Roxb:). On this kind of ground, after the soil has been ploughed for three times, and manured with ashes, these grains are sown broad-cast in the second month after the summer solstice. The seed is covered with a hoe, called *Ella-kudali*. The produce is much the same as *Bylu* land; but there are no means by which the extent of *Betta* ground can be estimated."

Buchanan also came to know about the prevalence of the *Cumri* (shifting cultivation) in the northern part of Canara.

> "**Cumri cultivation**. - In the hilly parts of the country, many people of a *Marattha* extraction use the *Cumri,* or *Cotu-cadu* cultivation. In the first season, after burning the woods, they sow *Ragy* (*Cynosurus*), *Tovary* (*Cytisus cajan*), and *Harulu* (*Ricinus*). Next year they have from the same ground a crop of *Shamay* (*Panicum miliare* Lamarck.). These hills are not private property, and pay no land-tax; but those who sow them pay, for the right of cultivation, a poll-tax of half a *Pagoda,* or nearly 4*s*. On account of poverty, many of them at present are exempted from this tax."

On 24th February, Buchanan travelled from *Hulledy-pura* and encamped on the south side of a river opposite to *Mirzee* (Mirjan). On the way, he passed through a place called *Cumty* (Kumta). On the south side of *Mirzee* was a plain intersected by a salt water creek. The soil of the plain which extended all the way from *Hulledy-pura* was very sandy. For a coss north of *Cumty,* the ground was high, with very little cultivation, but a greater part of it seemed to be fit for being formed into *Mackey* (rain-fed cultivation) or at least into *Betta* land. Between this place and the river was a very fine plain, called *Hegada* (Hegde), near which Buchanan had encamped.

On 25th February, 1801, Buchanan made a circular tour through the country east from *Mirzee* (Mirjan). He described the face of the country that he passed through as follows:

> **"Feb. 25. Face of the country**. – In the morning, having crossed the river, I took a circle of about six miles into the country east from *Mirzee*, in order to see some forests that spontaneously produce black pepper. The whole of the country through which I passed was hilly; but I met with several narrow vallies well watered, though not fully cultivated, owing to a want of inhabitants. Many of the hills were so barren, steep, and rocky, that I was soon forced to dismount from my horse, and proceed on foot. These hills consist entirely of naked *Laterite.* Other hills, which were those I sought after, were covered with stately forests."

Buchanan's visit to one of the natural pepper bearing forests of *Mirzee* has been described in an earlier chapter (*Chapter 6*). He did not come across teak around the forests of *Mirzee.* The wild nutmeg and cinnamon trees were commonly met with.

After returning from the tour through the forests near *Mirzee*, Buchanan proceeded to a place called *Hirigutty* (Hiregutti) on the same day (25th February, 1801). He passed through a country that was very barren, consisting of low hills covered with stunted trees.

On 26th February, Buchanan went to *Gaukarna.* Due to thick fog he could not see the country properly; but near the road it was a plain, consisting mostly of rice fields. At the western extremity of this plain was a ridge of low barren hills, which bent round to the sea.

On 28th February, Buchanan went to *Ancola.* Midway, he came across a river called *Gangawali.* Between *Gaukarna* and the river, the country consisted of low hills, separated by rice grounds of very small extent. Soon after leaving the *Gangawali* he crossed a smaller salt water inlet, which by overflowing it at high water used to injure a good deal of land. On 1st March, he went to a place called *Chandya.* On the way, he crossed a big salt water inlet called *Belicary.* The country between *Ancola* and *Chandya* was plain with good soil but in many places it was spoiled by the interruption of salt water creeks. Next day, Buchanan went to *Sedasiva-ghur* by a road that passed over two steep ridges of hills. The plain on the north of the two ridges was very sandy and much spoiled by sea water. A great part of the plain was a waste covered with bushes of *Cassuvium*, locally called *Govay*, introduced from America by the Portuguese of Goa. [**Note**: *Cassuvium* is the older name of cashew, or *Anacardium occidentale.*]

After halting at *Sedasiva-ghur* for a couple of days, Buchanan proceeded towards the *Ghats*. His first destination was *Gopi-chitty* (Gopshitta). He described the appearance of the country as follows:

> "**March 4. Appearance of the country.** – I went three cosses to *Gopi-chitty*. For the first part of the journey the road led through a level country, with a few small hills scattered at some distance, and a pretty good soil. It afterwards passed among low hills covered with wood. In many places here, the soil seems good, and the trees are tall; so that pepper might probably be cultivated to advantage. In many other places the hills are barren, producing nothing but bushes, or stunted trees: among them I saw no *Teak.* ----"

On 5th March, 1801, Buchanan proceeded to a place called *Caderi* (Kadra). On the way, he passed through many places that formerly had been cultivated but had become waste, and through some places where the soil seemed fit for cultivation but which probably had never been cleared. The trees in some places were of a good size, but none of them were valuable. On the basis of his observations and information provided by the local people, Buchanan described the tree species along with their principal uses and other characteristics. The list of trees comprising nineteen (19) species along with Buchanan's narration/comments has been appended at **Annexure III.**

On 6th March, 1801, Buchanan went to a place called *Avila-gotna*. The road passed through forests in the midst of which there were small scattered villages, hidden in the recesses. These forests were infested with numerous tigers. To lessen the danger of attack by these animals, the traders who used to frequent the road had cleared many places where they could encamp without fear. The cleared patches were prevented from being overgrown by annually burning the long grass. During his journey, Buchanan halted in one of these clear places. Buchanan's description about the appearance of the country, including his observations on the deciduous forest that he had passed through, is reproduced below.

> "**Appearance of the country**. – The country through which I passed to-day was in general level, with hills near the road toward the left, and a ridge to the right at about four or five miles distance. This ridge is that which runs out into the sea to form the southern boundary of *Sedasiva-ghur*. The trees are in general high, with many *Bamboos* intermixed. The soil is apparently good, and a large proportion of it is sufficiently level for the plough. Near *Avila-gotna* I crossed the river, which here assumes a very singular appearance. Its channel is about half a mile wide, and consists of a confused mass of rocks, gravel, and sand, intersected by small limpid streams, and overgrown with various trees and shrubs which delight in such situations. In the rainy season, it swells into tremendous torrents, but never fills the channel from bank to bank. It is then, however, quite impassable. At present its clear streams, with the fresh verdure of the plants growing near them, are very pleasant, after having come through the forest, whose leaves at this season drop; for all the juices of the trees are dried up by the arid heat of this climate, in the same manner as they are by the cold of an European winter. The nights, however, are at present cool, but the days are burning hot. Near the sea a more equable temperature prevails."

Next day, Buchanan went to a place called *Deva-kara* by a road that passed along the side of the river. Toward the east the valley became narrower and more uneven, but still much of it was fit for the plough. From the stunted appearance of the trees, Buchanan concluded that the soil was worse than that on the previous day's route. Buchanan had noticed that at *Deva-kara* a good deal of land had been cleared and formed into rice fields. However, the inhabitants of the village comprising only eight families were not enough to cultivate the whole.

On 8th March, 1801, Buchanan left *Deva-kara* and proceeded further. The road ran about two cosses near the river side, with stony hills to the right. From there, the road passed for half a coss through a forest of the kind which spontaneously produced black pepper. Beyond this he came to another valley watered by a perennial stream, and cultivated like the former. Afterwards Buchanan went about half a coss through a forest, where the ground was very level, and capable of being converted into rice fields. At the end of this, Buchanan entered a third valley, which was called *Barabuli*, and like the two former was finely watered, planted and cultivated. Buchanan camped at *Barabuli* for the day. Near *Barabuli*, Buchanan came across another forest with naturally occurring pepper vines. Buchanan described as below.

"----Near it is another hill that spontaneously produces pepper; and there are many such in this part of *Karnata*, especially in the *Yella-pura* and *Chinna-pura* districts. These pepper-hills are miserably neglected. The vines are not tied up to one third part of the trees, and the whole ground is overgrown with brush-wood. From their moisture a delightful freshness prevails in these places; and were they carefully cultivated, and the trees manured, I have no doubt, but that the pepper would be of a quality as good as any other. No tree should be allowed to grow in them, but such as are of some use; and of these the country spontaneously produces many; namely, two species of *Artocarpus*, *Teak*, blackwood, *Cassia*, wild-nutmegs, *Caryota urens*, and the *Bassia*, with perhaps some others that escaped my notice. At present, however, these valuable kinds are not numerous, for they are overwhelmed by such as are totally useless. By the natives these pepper forests are called *Maynasu Canu*. The people here have no idea that anything farther should be done to them, than once in three years to cut the bushes, and once annually to tie the vines to the young trees; and even these operations are much neglected. But, to make the most of such places, they ought to be carefully cultivated, no trees ought to be permitted to grow in them but such as are of use, and the vines ought to be manured as much as possible."

Buchanan was highly impressed with the forests that he passed through near *Barabuli*. He was particularly impressed with the matti (*Terminalia tomentosa*) trees. He wrote as follows (8th March, 1801):

> **"Mutti.** In all this day's journey, even where the soil was full of stones, the forests through which I passed were very stately. The *Mutti* (*Chuncoa Muttia* Buch: MSS.) in particular grows to a prodigious size. The natives use the ashes of its bark to eat with *Betel*, in the same manner as in other parts quick-lime is employed. Fewer of the trees lose their leaves here than nearer the sea; for a freshness and moisture are kept up by the vicinity of the mountains, which every morning are involved in the clouds."

On 9th March, 1801, Buchanan proceeded towards his next destination, *Cutaki*. After ascending close to the river, with a high hill immediately on his right, Buchanan came to the foot of the *Ghat*. He then ascended a very long and steep hill, sloping up by the sides of deep glens, and having gone a little way on a level ridge, he descended a considerable way into a valley which contained a perennial stream, rice ground, and a wood that spontaneously produced pepper, and which was totally neglected. He then ascended a mountain, still longer and steeper than the first, and after a very short descent came to a small lake, and a building for accommodation of travelers. After another short ascent, Buchanan arrived at a plain country above the *Ghats*, and immediately afterwards he reached *Cutaki* (Kattige).

Having reached the heart of the Western *Ghats*, Buchanan described the majesty of the forests of the region in the following words.

> **"March 9. Soil and trees of the western *Ghats*.** - Here the western *Ghats* assume an appearance very different from that at *Pedda Nayakana Durga*, or *Kaveri-pura*. The hills, although steep and stony, are by no means rugged, or broken with rocks: on the contrary, the stones are buried in a rich mould, and in many places are not to be seen without digging. Instead, therefore, of the naked, sun-burnt, rocky peaks, so common in the eastern *Ghats*, we here have fine mountains clothed with the most stately forests. I have no where

seen finer trees, nor any *Bamboos* that could be compared with those which I this day observed. The *Bamboos* compose a large part of the forest, grow in detached clumps, with open spaces between, and equal in height the *Caryota urens*, one of the most stately palms, of which also there is great plenty. There is no underwood nor creepers to interrupt the traveller who might choose to wander in any direction through these woods; but the numerous tigers, and the unhealthiness of the climate, would render any long stay very uncomfortable. About midway up the *Ghats* the *Teak* becomes common; but it is very inferior in size to the following trees which unfortunately are of less value."

Continuing with the above description Buchanan provided a list of nine tree species found in the forests along with their principal uses and other characteristics. The list of trees with Buchanan's narration/comments has been appended at **Annexure IV**.

On 10th March, 1801, Buchanan proceeded to *Yella-pura*. Buchanan's description of the appearance of the country including his thoughts on cultivating (nurturing) pepper in forest as also on clearing forest for taking up cultivation is reproduced below.

"**March 10. Appearance of the country**. – I went four cosses to *Yella-pura*. The first part of the road led through a forest spontaneously producing pepper. The trees and soil are very fine; but owing to a want of cultivators, according to the report of the inhabitants, not above one fourth of the pepper is procured from it that ought to be. This forest is intersected by narrow vallies of rice-ground, with a few gardens well supplied with water from springs and rivulets. I afterwards passed through a very hilly country; but the hills are of no considerable height, and in general the soil is apparently good. The trees, however, are not so large as where the pepper grows; and it is universally agreed, that the plant will not thrive in any forest but where it is found spontaneously growing. Many places among these hills are so level that the plough might be employed; and I suppose they might be cultivated for *Car' Ragy*, as is done in similar situations at *Priya-pattana*; but the people say, that unless the ground has been formed into terraces, the rains here are so heavy as to sweep away the seed. The rains in general are fully adequate to produce one crop of rice from any land properly levelled; and therefore it might be thought that by far the greater part of the country here might be cultivated for rice; but the people have an idea that no part of the country is fit for that purpose, but what has been already cultivated. Even of this, owing to a want of cultivators, three fourths are at present waste. The gardens being more profitable, and being also private property, are better occupied; and not above one-quarter of them have gone to ruin."

Next day, Buchanan proceeded to a place called *Caray Hossa-hully*. He described the face of the country and the richness and diversity of the forests that were met with in the following words.

"March 11. Face of the country. – I went four cosses to *Caray Hossa-hully*, that is, the new village at the tank. The whole country, so far as I saw, was totally uninhabited, and very few traces of former cultivation were observable. A few narrow vallies seem once to have been under rice. The higher grounds, I suspect, have been always a forest; although from the stateliness of the trees, the soil would appear to be good, and in its present state much of it is not too steep for the plough, while no part seems incapable of being formed into terraces, as is done below the *Ghats*. In a small portion near *Yella-pura*, the trees of the forest were stunted, and from a want of moisture had lost their leaves; but in the greater part they were very luxuriant, and many of the kinds were, to me at least, quite unknown. In my botanical investigations, however, I had very little success; for the cutting down one of these trees is a day's work for four or five natives; and at *Yella-pura* I could procure nobody that would climb to bring me specimens. The vast number of ants, indeed, that live on the trees in India, render this a very disagreeable employment."

On 12th March, 1801, Buchanan went to a place called *Sancada-gonda*. The whole country was covered with forest. The soil almost everywhere appeared to be excellent, with more low vallies, and more vestiges of former cultivation, than on the previous day's route. Next day (March 13, 1801), he went to a place called *Soonda*, or *Sudha*. The route was circuitous, and the hills were much steeper than those on the last two days route, and of course less fit for the cultivation of rice; but there were many deep and narrow vallies fit for *Betel-nut* gardens, and several of these were already under occupation and cultivation.

On 14th March, Buchanan went to *Sersi* (Sirsi) which was the residence of the *Tahsildar* of *Soonda* or *Sudha*. The road to *Sersi* was through a country which was more level than through which he came the previous day. In two places the trees of the forest were covered with pepper vines; but these were entirely neglected. After halting at *Sersi* for two days, he proceeded to *Banawasi* on 16th March, 1801. A great deal of the country through which he passed had been formerly cleared. Although most of these areas had become waste, they had not yet been overgrown with trees. The woods, being young, did not contain tall trees. However, at one place Buchanan passed through a stately forest, in which pepper-vine grew spontaneously. In this forest there was some *Teak*. The greater part of the country was not too steep for the plough; but in many places the *Laterite* rose to the surface. In other areas, the soil was apparently good.

On 18th March, 1801, after a halt of two days at *Banawasi*, Buchanan left Canara and entered the territory of Mysore State.

AN OVERVIEW OF THE FORESTS OF CANARA

From the above narration it is evident that Buchanan had undertaken a fairly extensive tour of Canara spanning about two months. His tour covered all the three distinct areas of Canara, namely, the coastal areas, the interior areas below the *Ghats*, and the areas above the *Ghats*. During his travel, Buchanan made it a point to describe the appearance or face of the country as he went from one place to the next. Such descriptions invariably contained his observations on the natural vegetation including tree growth on the landscape. On two occasions, Buchanan also described some of the tree species occurring in the forests that he had passed through. Buchanan's narrations and observations help us to some extent in visualizing the status of the forests of Canara during the beginning of the nineteenth century.

Buchanan had on two occasions mentioned about the prevalence of *Cumri* or shifting cultivation in the forests of Canara. In the southern parts of Canara (*Tulava* country), *Cumri* cultivation was carried out by an indigenous tribe called *Malekudia*, whereas in the northern parts of Canara it was done by people of a *Marattha* extraction. Towards the end of his tour of Canara, Buchanan had received a report from Mr. Read, collector of the northern division of Canara, providing a lot of information about various aspects of the division including land tenure, revenue, trade, export, import, etc. On the basis of Mr. Read's report, Buchanan in his diaries had included the following details of *Cumri* cultivation pertaining to that part of Canara situated below the *Ghats* and comprising the districts (*Talucs*) of *Kunda-pura*, *Honawera* and *Ancola*.

> "The number of people at present employed in the *Cumri*, or *Cotu-cadu* cultivation, amounts to 2418, who pay yearly 954½ *Pagodas*, or 3*s*. 2¼*d*. a head. It is supposed by the revenue officers, that in this manner 1900 more people might find employment."

Since Canara had been annexed by the British just about a decade earlier to the visit of Buchanan in 1801, the above details make it amply clear that shifting cultivation (*Cumri/Cotucadu*) was an established practice in Canara, being prevalent since a long time, and the existing practice was continued by the British after taking over the reins of administration. Besides, the large number (2418) of people who were reported to have practiced *Cumri* in the three taluks of Kundapur, Honnavar and Ankola is a pointer to the fact that large extents of forest area had already been brought under shifting cultivation by the beginning of the nineteenth century. It is also interesting to note that the Revenue administration of that time regarded *Cumri* as an avenue of employment which could also add to the revenue collection. Apparently, the evil effects of large-scale *Cumri* cultivation being carried out in the forest areas were yet to be recognized during the formative years of the British administration.

From Buchanan's narrations of the appearance of the country, it may be observed that on all the occasions when he had travelled along the coastal areas of Canara, he had passed through terrains comprising low hills, mostly lateritic and barren, sometimes with stunted trees or thorny bushes, in addition to gardens and rice-fields in the valleys. As a matter of fact, the entire coastal forest belt of Karnataka now harbors what is known as the Lateritic scrub forest, and what Buchanan had noticed about 220 years ago were stretches of such forest only. Originally these areas harbored evergreen forests. However, due to anthropogenic pressure, most notably shifting cultivation followed by continuous and excessive withdrawal of biomass, degradation of these forests had set in a long time ago; heavy rainfall subjected the opened-up areas to severe laterisation, eventually turning these into lateritic scrub capable of harboring very few hardy and/or thorny species. In the above process of forest degradation, the coastal areas were the hardest hit, as they were relatively more populated than the interior parts of Canara.

As regards the interior areas below the *Ghats*, Buchanan had visited a number of places in the southern part of Canara where he had noticed a mixed type of natural vegetation. While some areas had very good forest, some areas had newly emerging crop (perhaps post *Cumri*), some areas were cleared of wood, some areas had outcrop of granite or laterite, etc. In comparison, the interior parts of northern Canara below the *Ghats* were fairly well-wooded, many of these areas harboring spontaneously growing pepper vines. It may be noted that the interior parts of southern Canara below the *Ghats* were relatively more populated than the interior parts of northern Canara below the *Ghats*; as a result, the effects of *Cumri* and other biotic factors were more discernible in the southern part of interior Canara than those in the northern part of interior Canara.

As already mentioned, Buchanan came across fairly good forest in the interior parts of northern *Canara* below the *Ghats*. He came across very good forest above the *Ghats* also. While travelling through these forests, he identified the constituent tree species on two occasions. Near *Caderi* (Kadra) situated below the *Ghats* he had identified nineteen (19) tree species (**Annexure-III**), and near *Cutaki* (Kattige), just above the *Ghats*, he had identified nine (9) species (**Annexure-IV**). Perusal of these tree species would indicate that most of these were typical of deciduous forest while a few such as *Holigarna grahamii, Strychnos nux-vomica, Cinnamomum* species, *Michelia champaka,* and *Artocarpus lakucha* are normally associated with evergreen forest. Buchanan had also mentioned of a few more species including two species of *Artocarpus,* Nutmeg, *Caryota urens,* etc. near a place called *Barabuli.* All these tend to indicate that the forests the composition of which Buchanan had described were primarily semi-evergreen forests with relatively higher proportion of deciduous species, and some secondary moist deciduous forests.

Buchanan did not appear to have come across extensive areas of pure moist deciduous forest during his tour through Canara, because, in that eventuality he would have noticed and mentioned about total and large-scale leaf-shedding of trees during the course of his travel. It may also be noted that he did not see extensive teak forests in Canara except in a few places such as near *Cavila-cutty, Barabuli,* and *Banawasi,* where there were some teak trees. During his entire tour of Canara, Buchanan had come across only two patches of purely deciduous forest: first, on way to *Avila-gotna,* and then near *Yella-pura.* Since Buchanan's first phase of tour in the Mysore State was from June to October, he did not have an occasion to witness the phenomenon of total leaf-shedding of a purely deciduous forest. During his tour through southern Canara he mostly travelled through evergreen and semi-evergreen forests where the phenomenon of total leaf-shedding is not observed. Buchanan travelled through the northern part of Canara during the month of March which was the right time for total leaf-shedding of a purely deciduous forest. Buchanan had rightly observed this phenomenon in the two above-mentioned patches of deciduous forest near *Avila-gotna* and *Yella-pura* which were surrounded by evergreen or semi-evergreen forests. His observation that the trees in the patch of forest near *Yella-pura* were stunted can be attributed to the fact that this deciduous patch of forest perhaps comprised secondary deciduous growth, having retrograded from what originally was an evergreen forest.

During his tour, especially in northern Canara, both below and above the *Ghats,* Buchanan on many occasions had come across forests growing spontaneous pepper vine. In reality, these were tropical wet evergreen forests. These forests come up where the soil is very rich and the rainfall is copious. Naturally growing pepper vines are very commonly met with in these forests. As these forests harbor more softwood and only a few hardwood trees, in terms of timber production they were considered useless as compared with the deciduous and semi-evergreen forests. As black pepper was an important spice both for local consumption and export, people in certain parts of Canara used to nurture the naturally growing pepper vines in the forest and harvest abundant crop. This practice has been discussed in some detail in a preceding chapter (*Chapter 6*). In the initial years of their administration, the British considered this practice as an ideal land-use of an area that was otherwise considered as useless. Therefore, in order to boost production of black pepper they encouraged people to take up cultivation (nurturing) of the naturally occurring pepper vines in the forest areas. During his tour, Buchanan had often commented upon this practice not being carried out properly by the people. In the Nagara region of Mysore State where similar forests were met with, Buchanan was surprised to find that the practice of cultivating (nurturing) pepper vine in the forest areas was not at all prevalent. He considered this as neglect of the forests.

It is interesting to note that while travelling from *Sersi* to *Banawasi* Buchanan had passed through a stately forest in which pepper-vine grew spontaneously and there were some teak trees also. Teak trees primarily grow in deciduous forest and the natural occurrence of teak in an evergreen forest is very unlikely. However, in the midst of the deciduous forests of *Banawasi*, we come across some special pockets containing evergreen forest. These special pockets of evergreen forest are known as *Kan* lands. What Buchanan had seen on way to *Banawasi* was probably such a Kan land which was surrounded by a deciduous forest harboring some teak trees. Such *Kan* lands also occur in the adjoining taluks of Soraba, Shikaripur, Sagar, and Hosanagara of the Shivamogga district.

It is significant that Buchanan mentioned about most of the important hardwood timber species of Canara, besides a few medium hardwood species. Most of the species he described, with the exception of a few, are deciduous tree species. Although he was an accomplished botanist, he did not appear to have evinced much interest in exploring the evergreen forests of Canara through which he had passed during his travel. This was perhaps due to paucity of time and also owing to the fact that during those days softwood timber was not at all in demand. His interest in some of the evergreen trees such as Cinnamon and Nutmeg was primarily because of the importance of these trees as source of spices.

STATUS AND OWNERSHIP OF FOREST LAND

We have mentioned earlier that the concept of forest as a distinct administrative entity was not in existence in the distant past. Even after the system of land tenure based on land-use evolved, forest did not automatically find place in such tenures. In this context, a query raised by Buchanan and the answer to the query given by Mr. Ravenshaw, the collector of the southern division of Canara, are reproduced below.

> **"Query 1**st. What proportion of your district consists of land that has always been uncultivated? Of this, what part might, with proper management, be converted into rice-ground? What part into coco-nut or *Betel-nut* gardens? What proportion of this waste land is now cleared for grass, what is under forest, and what is enclosed for plantations of timber trees, firewood, &c.

> **"Answer.** No account of the extent of jungles (forests) has ever been taken. All the surveys that have been made only went to ascertain the cultivated lands, and those capable of culture, but not at present cultivated, and which are 111,965½ *Morays*. Of this, 24,181 *Morays* are cleared for grass, 7,043 have a capability of being converted into rice ground, and 1,789 are fit for gardens. No account is kept of the quantity enclosed for timber, but all the remainder would answer for the purpose. N. B. The average *Moray* is 45 *Guntas*, each 33 square, or 49,005 square feet and is therefore nearly 1 13/100 acre."

The above reply indicates that no specific area was earmarked as forest. What we understand today as forest was a sub-set of a general term called wastelands. In the report that Mr. Read, the collector of the northern division of Canara, had submitted to Buchanan, the word wastelands had been used to indicate the areas from which various forest products had been procured.

As regards ownership of forest lands, there appears to have been some differences in different parts of Canara. During his stay at Mangalore, Buchanan was informed that all the lands of *Tulava* were private property: 'In *Tulava* the state has no lands; the whole is private property. All the land-tax is now paid in money; but before the conquest part of it was demanded in rice, and other articles of consumption for the troops, at a low rate, which was fixed by the officers of government'. While describing the manner of *Cumri* cultivation by the *Malay-cudies*, Buchanan had once again reiterated the status of ownership of land as follows: 'In this neighbourhood, the hills that are cultivated after the *Cotucadu* or *Cumri* manner are all private property. The *Mulucaras*, or proprietors, have alienated the whole right of cultivating them to a rude tribe, called *Malayar*, or *Malay-cudies*'.

During his stay at *Hulledy-pura*, Buchanan had commented that 'Most of the cultivated lands in *Haiga* are private property; but the hills and forests belong to the government'. He had also indicated that even the people who carried out *Cumri* in forest areas had to pay tax: 'These hills are not private property, and pay no land-tax; but those who sow them pay, for the right of cultivation, a poll-tax of half a *Pagoda*, or nearly 4*s*.' Buchanan had also quoted from Mr. Read's report regarding levy of tax from people who were allowed to do *Cumri* in the forest lands. What Buchanan was implying through these comments/observations was that forest lands were a property of the government.

However, Buchanan had also mentioned about people's perceptions about forest lands. During his tour in the forest near *Mirzee* (25th February, 1801), Buchanan had remarked: 'The landlords (*Malugaras*) pretend, that all the timber trees are their property, but none of them are saleable'. Again, while visiting the forest near *Caderi* (Kadra) on 5th March, 1801, Buchanan had commented as follows:

> "The forests are the property of the gods of the villages in which they are situated, and the trees ought not to be cut without having obtained leave from the *Gauda*, or head man of the village, whose office is hereditary, and who here also is the priest (*Pujari*) to the

temple of the village god. The idol receives nothing for granting this permission; but the neglect of the ceremony of asking his leave brings his vengeance on the guilty person. This seems, therefore, merely a contrivance to prevent the government from claiming the property. Each village has a different god, some male, some female, but by the *Brahmans* they are all called *Saktis* (powers), as requiring bloody sacrifices to appease their wrath."

Chapter 11

CONCLUSION

Buchanan had visited Mysore and Canara in the aftermath of a series of closely fought wars which had left a trail of devastation on the landscape of the regions. A number of invasions by marauding armies had inflicted immense damages to the lives and properties of the people causing untold miseries. Droughts, followed by famines, were frequent especially in greater part of the Mysore State. Frequent wars had resulted in very heavy tax burden, bordering on extortion. All these had adversely impacted the population, the most severely affected among them being the farmers many of whom had abandoned their cultivations. With the hint of an assurance of relative political stability, people were slowly coming back and resuming their normal agricultural activities and other occupations.

As agriculture and related activities constituted the backbone of the economy of that period, Buchanan had devoted considerable part of his time in seeing and understanding the status of agriculture in different parts of Mysore and Canara. In the course of his journey, while he had witnessed the grim scenario of an almost collapsed agricultural infrastructure, he had also noticed the resilient farmer picking up the threads and starting life all over again. What impressed him was the farmer's ability to wisely use the available resources including scarce water to raise various crops in accordance with the capability of the land that he had possessed. Even in the vestiges of what once were flourishing agricultural fields, Buchanan could discern tit bits of the best practices that the farmers had been adopting since ages, such as planting of the *babul* or *karijali* trees on the borders of farmlands or forming tall and secure hedges of *Euphorbium tirucalli*.

Throughout his travel, Buchanan had closely observed the agricultural practices followed by the farmers in different parts of Mysore and Canara. During those days, the method of farming was purely organic. Chemical fertilizer was unknown anywhere in the world. While cow dung was the most important manure, it was not enough for all the lands; the quantity of manure was augmented by mixing the cow dung with dry grass, green grass, dry leaves, green leaves, domestic wastes, etc. depending upon what were available in different seasons of the year. Buchanan had noticed a very significant role that the farmers had assigned to trees and other plants to complement their agricultural operations. In fact there was an intrinsic relationship between water, agricultural crops, and trees or other plants. There was a conscious attempt at conserving water, increasing soil organic content and improving soil fertility with the help of trees and other plants. Buchanan in his descriptions had highlighted the various ways of preparation and use of manure by the farmers and also about the various types of fences that were raised around the farmlands not only as a means of physical protection of the crops but also for ensuring conservation of soil and water in the farmlands. Buchanan was so convinced about the benefits of the above organic ways of improving soil fertility and conserving soil and moisture in farmlands that he was quite dismayed to find that these measures were not being adopted properly in certain parts of Mysore, such as in some of the areas that represent the present districts of Shivamogga, Davanagere, Chitradurga, and Hassan.

Buchanan had noticed that a greater part of the Mysore State was bereft of good natural vegetation. He often mentioned about frequent occurrences of drought-like conditions due to 'a want of the rain'. Despite such near arid conditions, however, the farmers were able to raise crops of rice, sugar-cane, betel-nut and betel-leaf even in places like Madhugiri, Sira, Chikkanayakanahalli, Kolar, etc. This was possible partly because of their wise use of land and measured use of the available water, and partly because of the various ingenious ways that they had devised to keep the earth cool. For this, they made excellent use of whatever limited plant resources were available in the neighbourhood at their disposal, be it *Dodonaea viscosa*, *Argemone mexicana*, *Datura metel*, *Leucas aspera*, or *Calotropis gigantea*. The meticulous way in which the farmers used to raise the areca-nut gardens in a phased manner by gradually creating a cooler ambience necessary for areca plants is an example of their perfect understanding about the relationship between crop and the surrounding natural environment.

Among the various messages which Buchanan's writings convey, the most pertinent one for the present times is perhaps that of the ancient wisdom of the farmer that the surest way to keep the earth cool is to keep it green. No matter what we write or profess about containing global warming, the actual theatre for action has to be in agricultural lands which constitute the largest segment of land use in the State. Overall, agricultural lands constitute about 65 per cent of the geographical area of the State of Karnataka. In the Eastern Plains and interior Karnataka, where the degree of aridity is significantly palpable and the signs of desertification are already visible in certain parts, the proportion of agricultural lands to that of the geographical area is even higher, ranging from 80 to 90 per cent. While attempts to protect and expand the forest and tree cover in public lands including forest lands must continue, greening of the agricultural lands will have a more salutary effect on the ambient temperature of the surrounding environment. Here it must be reiterated that greening of agricultural lands is not to reduce but to complement agricultural productivity. It is a well-known fact that the available water capacity (AWC) or the water holding capacity of at least 40 per cent of Karnataka's agricultural lands is below the threshold limit prescribed for long duration crops. These areas are more ideal for agroforestry or dry land horticulture. Tree planting in one form or another is the only way to improve the water holding capacity of these parched lands. It will also help in providing a platform for integrated farming systems (IFS) which will enable farmers to pursue a number of complementary and mutually beneficial activities such as agriculture, horticulture, agroforestry, animal husbandry, sericulture, apiculture, pisciculture, etc.

TREES OF THE SAVANA-DURGA FORESTS AS MENTIONED BY BUCHANAN

While travelling from Srirangapatna (*Seringapatam*) to Bangalore, Buchanan had passed through the forests of *Savana-durga* in Magadi (June 15-19, 1800). He gave a detailed account of the trees that chiefly composed the forests and their important uses. The names of the trees as given by Buchanan and his comments are reproduced in the 2nd and 3rd columns of the following table.

Sl. No.	Present scientific and local names	Local and scientific names used by Buchanan	Comments of Buchanan
(1)	(2)	(3)	(4)
1	*Ixora arborea* (gorivi)	*Henna Gorivi, Ixora arborea,* Roxb. MSS.	A small tree used for beams and posts in the houses of the poorer natives. People travelling at night use pieces of it for torches, as it burns readily and clearly.

2	An unidentified species of *Ixora*	*Ghendu Gorivi*, or *Haydarany.*	Serves for the same purposes as the preceding, and is probably a species of the same genus.
3	*Terminalia tomentosa* (Matti)	*Cari Hulivay? Clutia forte stipularis?*	I believe the natives misapplied this name. They had often mentioned it to me, and had brought a specimen of the timber; but in the woods they sometimes called one tree by this name, and sometimes another. At last they fixed positively on this, which is said to produce good timber.
4	*Terminalia paniculata* (Kindal/Hunal)	*Heb*, or *Bily Hulivay, Chuncoa Huliva*, Buch. MSS.	A large tree, and good timber.
5	*Terminalia arjuna* (Torematti/ Holematti) Also *Terminalia tomentosa* (matti)	*Tor Mutti, Chuncoa Muttea*, Buch. MSS.	At *Chinapatam* this tree is called *Cari Hulivay*. To the northward it is commonly called *Muddi*, which is a *Telinga* name. It is a very large tree, and its timber is very useful.
6	*Terminalia bellirica* (Tare)	*Tari, Myrobalanus Taria*, Buch. MSS.	Is a large tree much used by the natives. Its timber becomes tolerably durable, if, after being cut, it be kept some months under water. The kernel of the fruit is esculent.

7	*Terminalia chebula* (Alale/ Harda)	*Arulay, Myrobalanus Arula*, Buch. MSS.	The timber of this tree, like that of the former, requires to be watered in order to render it durable. The fruit is the common tanning and dyeing *myrobalan* of this country.
8	*Spondias mangifera* (Amte) or *Lannea coromandelica* (Godda)	*Amutty*, or *Gowda?*	It grows to be a large tree, and its timber is used for planks, beams, and posts.
9	*Diospyros montana* (jagalaganti)	*Jugalagunti, Diospyros montana*, Roxb.	The timber of this tree is said to be hard, and durable; but from some prejudice, it is never used by the natives. Its name signifies the *scolding wife*.
10	*Diospyros melanoxylon* (Tupra/Tumri)	*Tupru, Diospyros Tupru*, Buch. MSS.	Used for small beams and posts. The timber is said to be very hard and strong.
11	*Bauhinia* species (Basavanapada)	*Vana Raja*, or *Asha, Bauhinia.*	It is called the prince of the forest, on account of the superior excellence of its timber; but it does not grow to a large size.
12	*Dalbergia lanceolaria* (Hasaruganni/ Bilibeete)	*Hassur Gunny, Dalbergia?*	Grows to a middling size, and its timber is good; it nearly resembles the following tree; but may be readily distinguished by the bottom of its leaflets being acute; while in the other they are rounded.

13	*Dalbergia paniculata* (Pachali/Padri)	*Pachery, Dalbergia paniculata*, Rox.	Grows to a large size, but its timber is very useless; for the layers of which it is composed readily separate.
14	*Dalbergia latifolia* (beete/ sissum)	*Biridy, Pterocarpus Sissoo*, Roxb. MSS.	A middling sized tree of an excellent quality for furniture. By the Mussulmans it is called *Sissoo*; but it does not seem to be exactly the same with the tree of that name which grows in the north of India.
15	*Pterocarpus marsupium* (Honne)	*Whonay, Pterocarpus santalinus, L. F.*	A large good timber tree, fit for furniture. Its bark contains a blood-coloured juice.
16	*Pongamia pinnata* (Honge)	*Hoingay, Robinia mitis* Lin.	It grows to be a large tree, and its timber becomes tolerably durable; if, after it has been cut, it be kept some months in water.
17	*Chloroxylon swietenia* (Hurugalu/ Mashawal)	*Hurugulu, Chloroxylon quod Swietenia chloroxylon,* Roxb.	This never grows to be a large tree, and its timber is beautiful. It is said to be the satin wood of the English cabinet-makers.
18	*Boswellia serrata* (Dhupa)	*Chadacalu, Chloroxylon Dupada,* Buch. MSS.	An elegant tree, producing a resin that is frequently used in the temples, as incense.
19	*Soymida febrifuga* (Some)	*Swamy, Swietenia febrifuga,* Roxb. MSS.	A strong, but small timber tree, produces a fine clear gum.

20	*Chukrasia tabularis* (Kalgarike)	*Gowda, Sweitenia trilocularis,* Roxb. MSS.	A large tree; but its timber is very bad. Another tree, as before mentioned, was by the woodmen called *Gowda*, but that probably is a mistake.
21	*Grewia* species (Janiru)	*Jani, Grewia.*	There are three species called by this name, the *Asiatica*, the *Orientalis*, and that which I have named *Jania*. The timber of none of them is useful.
22	*Givotia rottleriformis* (Bilitale/Butala/ Tella Polki)	*Bili Tali, Bilitalium farinosum*, Buch. MSS.	In the *Telinga* language this tree is called *Tellamaliki*. It grows to a large size, and its timber was said to be good; but I found it to be white, soft, and very perishable.
23	*Cochlospermum gossipium/ religiosum* (Bettatavare/ Kadaburuga)	*Betta Tali*, or *Betta Tovary, Bombax gossyppinum.*	A large tree. Its timber becomes somewhat durable, if kept in water for some time after being cut; but without this precaution it is little worth.
24	An unidentified species	*Nai*, or *Cag Neralu.*	This cannot be of the same genus with the following *Nerulu*, as it has alternate serrated leaves. A large tree, the timber of which is much used.
25	*Syzygium cumini* (Neralu)	*Rudrashu Nerulu, Calyptranthes Jambulana* Willd.	Also much used. This is the tree from whence the *Brahmans* derive the name of the earth.

26	*Stereospermum chelonoides* (Padiri)	*Betta Padri, Bignonia chelonoides.*	A small tree; but its timber makes strong posts and beams.
27	*Dolichandrone falcata* (Wudige/ Godmurki)	*Wullay Padri, Bignonia spathacea.*	Timber little used.
28	*Vitex altissima* (Naviladi/ Bharanige)	*Navulady, Mail elou,* Hort. Mal. V. t. 1.	A large tree, and durable timber, which takes a polish, and is used for furniture, planks, beams, and posts.
29	*Gmelina arborea* (Shivani) (possibly)	*Shivuli,*	A small but good timber tree.
30	*Acacia leucophloea* (Bilijali/Topala)	*Topala, Mimosa leucophlea,* Roxb.	The bark, when newly cut, has a strong disagreeable smell, like that of *Mimosa Indica,* E. M. It grows to be a large tree, and produces strong timber for posts and beams. The bark is used by the natives in distilling spirit from *Jagory.*
31	*Acacia sundra/ chundra* (Kaggali)	*Cagali, Mimosa catechu,* Roxb. Pl. Cor. N. 174.	In some places, as near *Chinapatam,* this grows to be a large crooked tree. The quality of the timber is good. It is not the tree which produces the *Catechu.*
32	*Acacia suma,* mugali	*Mugli, Mimosa Covalum,* Buch. MSS.	A large tree. Timber black, very strong, and fit for posts and beams; but, like that of the foregoing, I was told, does not take a polish. This last report of the natives seems to be ill founded.

33	*Albizia amara* (Sujalu/tugli)	*Wullay Sujalu, Mimosa Tuggula,* Buch. MSS.	A large tree, but its timber is said to be not durable. To judge from appearance, however, this seems to be an error.
34	*Albizia odoratissima* (Bilwara/ Goddahunase)	*Betta Sujalu, Mimosa odoratissima,* L.	This is a large tree, which, according to the report of the woodmen, produces excellent durable timber.
35	*Ficus* species, perhaps *Ficus bengalensis* (Ala)	*Shalay, Ficus.*	Used for beams, and pillars of small size.
36	*Ficus glomerata* (Atti)	*Atty, Ficus glomerata,* Rox.	A large, useful tree. Its wood is remarkably light.
37	*Ficus carica* (Kalatti)	*Cull Atty, Ficus rupestris,* Buch. MSS.	In a good soil grows to a large size, but soon divides into branches. It is used for beams, posts, and planks.
38	*Ficus infectoria* (Basari)	*Birsi, Ficus.*	A large, useless tree.
39	*Erythroxylon monogynum* (Devadari)	*Devadarum, Erythroxylon sideroxylloides,* E. M.	Never grows to a large size; but its wood is odorous, durable, and capable of a polish. It is used by the poor instead of *sandal-wood*.

40	*Santalum album* (Srigandha)	*Sri Gunda, Santalum album.* *Sandal-wood* of the English merchants.	All the trees that were fit for sale have been lately cut by a *Brahman*, who was sent on purpose from *Seringapatam*. He procured about three thousand trees; but in less than ten years no more will be fit for cutting. The common size of the tree at the root, when it is cut, is about nine inches in diameter; but it has been known to arrive at a circumference of three cubits. In either case, not above a third of the diameter of the tree is of value; the remainder is white wood, totally devoid of smell. The wood is of the best quality in trees that have grown on a steep rocky soil; that which grows in low rich situations produces wood of little value. The trees were cut partly by the servants of the *Brahman*, and partly by woodmen hired on the spot. The branches and white wood were removed in the woods, and the billets were brought hither, and dried in the shade. Although the bottom of the stem, under the ground and immediately above the division into roots, is the most valuable part

			of the tree, no pains were taken to procure this, and the trees were cut above the surface of the soil. This want of economy is said to have proceeded from the stony nature of the soil; but this I doubt. Every thing relative to the price, market, or customs upon *sandal-wood* are here unknown; and the person who cut it was not under the authority of the *Amildar*. At two places in this hilly country the tree comes to great perfection; namely, at *Jalamangala*, between *Magadi* and *Chinapatam;* and at *Mutati Habigay*, near *Capala-durga*.
41	*Shorea talura* (Jalari)	*Jala, Shorea Jala*, Buch. MSS.	Here it grows only to a small size; but at *Rama-giri*, and many other places, it becomes large. It is said to take a polish, to be durable, and to be used for furniture. In *Mysore* it is on this tree only that the *Lac* insects breed. Formerly there were many trees near *Rama-giri* that contained *Lac*, and paid a considerable rent; but during the war carried on by Lord Cornwallis they were destroyed by the armies. Although there are

			now great numbers of the trees, none of the insects are reared. This is attributed to the want of leases. The *Amildar* was wont to let the trees for no longer than one year; it can therefore be no object for an individual to supply the trees with insects, as he would not be certain of enjoying the fruits of his labour. Some settled bargain for a number of years ought to be entered into with those who are willing to introduce such a valuable article of cultivation.
42	*Anogeissus latifolia* (Dindiga/ Dindal)	*Dinduga, Andersonia Panchmoum,* Roxb. MSS.	A large valuable timber tree, that is used for planks, beams, pillars, and furniture. It abounds in gum, and is nearly allied to the *Conocarpus* of botanists.
43	*Tectona grandis* (Thega)	*Doda Tayca, Tectona robusta.*	A few trees of this valuable timber are found in most places of this hilly tract; but in general they do not grow to be of a size sufficient for use. Some good timber may, it is said, be procured at *Mutati Habigay*, a place near *Capala-durga*.

44	*Adina cordifolia* (Heddi/Yethega)	*Ursina Tayca, Nauclea cordifolia*, Roxb.	Grows to be a large tree; and its timber is said to be equally valuable with that of the *Tectona*, or common *Teak*.
45	*Anthocephalus chinensis* (Kadamba/ Apate)	*Cadaga, Cadaba, or Cadava, Nauclea purpurea*, Roxb.	A large tree, the timber of which is much used.
46	*Lagerstroemia parviflora* (Channangi)	*Chaningy, Lagerstroemia parviflora*, Roxb.	In favourable situations it also grows to a large size; but its timber is of very little value. It may be improved, however, by soaking it in water for some months after it has been cut.
47	*Cordia macleodii* (Hadaga/ Hadang)	*Hadaga.*	A small tree; but its timber is used for furniture, door frames, and other purposes which require strong materials.
48	*Streblus asper* (Mitli)	*Mitly, Trophis aspera* Koenigii.	A small tree; but its timber is much esteemed on account of its being hard, and taking a good polish.
49	*Premna tomentosa* (Ije/ Narave)	*Easy, Premna tomentosa.*	Reported to be bad timber; but apparently without foundation. It is put as a frame work in the middle of mud walls in order to give them strength.

50	*Melia azadirachta.* (Bevu/Neem)	*Bewu, Melia azadirachta.*	A large timber tree, that is much used here, and from which a gum exudes.
51	*Wrightia tinctoria* (Hale/Beppale)	*Mara halay, Nerium tinctorium*, Roxb. MSS.	The natives are acquainted with its dyeing quality. Its timber is said to be hard, and white like ivory, and is used for small furniture, such as beds and chairs.
52	*Holoptelia integrifolia* (Tapasi)	*Tapissa, Ulmus integrifolia,* Roxb.	It is a small tree, but makes beams, planks, and posts.
53	*Zizyphus jujuba* (Elachi/Bore)	*Elichi, Rhamnus jujuba*, L.	Grows crooked; but its timber is hard, and is used for small furniture.
54	*Saccopetalum tomentosum* (Hessare/Omb)	*Heb Hessary, Uvaria tomentosa*, Roxb.	A small tree that is also used for furniture.
55	*Polyalthia cerasoides* (Sanna Hessare/Hoom)	*Chica Hessary, Uvaria cerasoides*, Roxb.	Useless.
56	*Aegle marmelos* (Bilva/Patri)	*Timbu Bayala, Egle marmelos*, Roxb.	A large tree, producing strong timber.
57	*Limonia crenulata* (Nai bela)	*Nai bayla, Limonia crenulata*, Roxb.	Useless.

| 58 | *Bambusa bambos* (Dowga) and *Dendrocalamus strictus* (Medri) | *Bideru, Bambusa.* | The *Bamboo* here is divided into two kinds: one solid, or nearly so, and is called by the natives *Chittu;* the other hollow, and called *Doda.* They are not considered as distinct species, the solidity of the former being attributed to its slow growth in dry stony places. Not having had an opportunity of examining the fructification, I cannot determine how far this opinion is well founded. It is the only kind found among these hills; and, although not of great size, is very strong and heavy. For common purposes I do not think it is so useful as the hollow kind; but it is admirably adapted for the shafts of spears, and by *Tippoo* was applied to that use for his cavalry. |
| 59 | *Buchanania angustifolia* (Murkal/ Maradi) | *Muruculu, Chirongia glabra,* Buch. MSS. | In many parts, and especially near *Chinapatam,* this is the most common tree. Its wood is not much valued; but it produces large quantities of a dark-coloured gum. The fruit is esculent. |

60	*Antidesma zeylanicum* (Amathi)	*Hulu Muruculu, Antidesma alexiteria.*	Of no use.
61	*Atalantia monophylla* (Kadunimbe)	*Cadu Nimbay*, or *Cadimbay.*	A small tree, that produces very hard timber fit for bolts, and small beams.
62	*Cordia monoica* (Panugeri)	*Narwully, Cordia monoica*, Roxb.	Ropes are made of its bark. The fruit is esculent, but tasteless.
63/64	*Gardenia latifolia* (Kambi) and another species of *Gardenia*	*Cambi, Gardenia* *Hay Cambi, Gardenia latifolia*, Roxb.	These two trees are useless.
65	*Jatropha curcas* (Mara haralu)	*Mara Haralu, Jatropa curcas.*	Its seed is collected for lamp oil. The dried stems answer excellently for match, as they burn slowly, and without flame.
66	*Semecarpus anacardium* (Kadgeru/ Gheru)	*Gheru, Anacardium semecarpus.*	The fruit used in medicine, and for marking linen. The timber is useless.
67	*Ochna obtusata* (Mudamara)	*Mudali, Ochna squarrosa.*	A beautiful but useless tree.
68	*Emblica officinalis* (Nelli)	*Nelli, Phyllanthus emblica.*	The timber is bad, yet the poor use it for beams and rafters. The fruit is pickled.
69	*Cassia fistula* (Kakke)	*Cacay, Cassia fistula.*	Used in religious ceremonies.
70	*Strychnos potatorum* (Chilla/Chitta)	*Chillu, Strychnos potatorum* Koenigii.	The timber useless. The use of the fruit, in cleaning water, is known to the natives.

"It must be observed, that the account I have given of the qualities of the timber trees is derived from the natives. I have had no opportunity yet of ascertaining their nature by experiments; but I have procured specimens of most of them; and from these specimens their real qualities may be hereafter determined. For this purpose, they have been transmitted to the Honourable Court of Directors, in whose Museum they have been deposited."

TREES OF THE HD KOTE FORESTS AS MENTIONED BY BUCHANAN

Buchanan had provided details of trees found in the forests in the foothills of the Western *Ghats* near *Hegodu Devana Cotay* (presently HD Kote) which he visited during September 16 -18, 1800. The names of the trees as given by Buchanan and his comments are reproduced in the 3rd and 4th columns of the following table:

Sl. No.	Present scientific and local names	Local and scientific names used by Buchanan	Comments of Buchanan
(1)	(2)	(3)	(4)
1	*Tectona grandis* (Thyega)	*Doda Tayca. Tectona robusta.*	In great plenty.
2	*Mitragyna parviflora* (kalam)	*Cadaba. Nauclea parvifolia* Roxb.	These two species, although very distinct, are by the woodmen of this place included under the same name. Both grow to a large size, and their timber is reckoned equal to that of *Teak,* or more properly *Tayca.*
3	*Adina cordifolia* (Heddi/Yethega)	*Nauclea cordifolia* Roxb.	

4	*Pterocarpus marsupium* (Honne)	*Honnay*, or *Whonnay*. *Pterocarpus santalinus*.	Is found in great plenty, and is a beautiful and useful tree.
5	*Dalbergia latifolia* (beete/sissum)	*Biriday, Pterocarpus*.	This is the same kind of tree with that of *Magadi*. By the Mussulmans it is called *Sissu*.
6	*Dalbergia paniculata* (Pachali/Padri)	*Dalbergia paniculata* Roxb.	Being useless, it has obtained no native name.
7	*Acacia catechu* (Kutch)	*Cagali. Mimosa Catechu* Roxb. Fl. Cor. No. 174.	Grows in the skirts of the forest only, and never reaches to a large size.
8	*Acacia ferruginea* (Banni)	*Bunni. Mimosa*.	This is very like the *Cagali*. Its timber is of no use. The tree is esteemed holy, as the shaft of *Rama's* spear is said to have been made of its wood.
9	*Albizia odoratissima* (Bilwara/ Goddahunase)	*Biluara. Mimosa odoratissima*.	At *Magadi* this tree was called *Betta Sujalu*. It is a large valuable timber-tree.
10	*Terminalia tomentosa* (Matti)	*Mutti. Chuncoa Muttea* Buch. MSS.	The natives here have several apellations which they give to this species; such as *Cari*, or black; *Bily*, or white; and *Tor*, by which name I knew it at *Magadi*.

11	*Terminalia chebula* (Alale/Harda)	*Alalay. Myrobalanus Arula* Buch. MSS.	Grows to a very large size; but the fruit, or *myrobalans*, are the only valuable part; and, owing to the remote situation of the place, these are not collected.
12	*Terminalia paniculata* (hunal/huluve/kindal)	*Hulivay. Chuncoa Huliva* Buch. MSS.	There is only one kind of this tree, although it has a great variety of names given to it by the natives. It is a large tree, and its timber is good.
13	*Terminalia bellirica* (Tari/Ghoting)	*Tari. Myroballanus Taria* Buch. MSS.	Very large.
14	*Acacia leucophloea* (Bilijali/Topala)	*Nai Bayla. Mimosa leucophlea* Roxb.	
15	*Buchanania lanzan* (Murkal/Nurkal)	*Muruculu. Chirongia sapida* Roxb. MSS.	These two trees, although they are lofty, do not grow to a great thickness. The woodmen talk of *Hen* and *Ghindu Muruculu*, or female and male; but they do it without precision, and do not apply one term to the one species, and another to the other.
16	*Buchanania angustifolia* (Maradi/Murkal)	*Chirongia glabra* Buch. MSS.	

17	*Eriolaena quinquelocularis* (Goomchi/ Gomajjige/ Kondigida/ Katale)	*Gumshia. Gumsia chloroxylon* Buch. MSS.	It does not grow to a large size; but the timber is said to be very strong, and has a singular green colour. Ropes are made of its bark.
18	*Anogeissus latifolia* (Dindiga/Dindal)	*Dinduga. Andersonia Panchmoun* Roxb. MSS.	Grows to a very large size. Its timber is valuable.
19	*Schleichera oleosa* (Kusum/Sagadi)	*Shagudda. Shaguda Cussum* Buch. MSS.	A large tree. Its timber, being very rarely found sound at heart, is not much esteemed.
20	*Semecarpus anacardium* (Kadgeru/Gheru)	*Gheru. Anacardium* Juss.	It is the fruit only of these two trees that is of any use.
21	*Emblica officinalis* (Nelli/Amla)	*Nelli, Phylanthus Emblica.*	
22	*Bridelia stipularis* (Goje)	*Goja. Clutia stipularis?*	A large tree, of which the timber is reckoned good.
23	*Elaeodendron glaucum* (Mukarki)	*Schrebera albens* Willd.	Has here no name. It is in fact, an *Eleodendrum*.
24	*Diospyros melanoxylon* (Tupra/Tumri)	*Tupru. Diospyros* Buch. MSS.	Here it is always a large tree, and its timber is esteemed good.
25	*Diospyros montana* (Jagalaganti)	*Jugalagunti. Diospyros.*	The same prejudice prevails here, as at *Magadi*, against this tree.

26	*Gmelina arborea* (Shivani)	*Culi.*	A large tree producing good timber.
27	*Bassia latifolia* (Ippe/Hal-tumri)	*Cad' Ipay. Bassia.*	The leaves are different in size and shape from those of *Bassia longifolia*, which is planted near villages. The art of extracting a spirituous liquor from the flowers is here unknown.
28	*Syzygium cumini* (Neral)	*Naerulu. Calyptranthes Jambulana* Willd.	
29	*Careya arborea* (Kaval/Kumbi)	*Gaula. Pelou* Hort. Mal.	The fruit is said to be as large as that of the *Artocarpus integrifolia*, and to be a favourite food with the elephant.
30	An unidentified species	*Budigayray.*	The fruit is said to poison fish.
31	*Vitex altissima* (Naviladi/ Bharanige)	*Navulady. Vitex alata* Buch. MSS.	A large timber tree.
32	*Shorea talura* (Jalari)	*Jala. Shorea Jala* Buch. MSS.	A large timber tree. No *lac* is made here.
33	An unidentified species	*Nirany.*	An useless tree.
34	*Ixora arborea* (Gorivi)	*Gurivi. Ixora arborea* Roxb. MSS.	Used for torches.

35	*Schrebera swietenioides* (Ghanthemara)	*Wudi. Schrebera Swietenioides* Roxb.	A large tree.
36	*Bauhinia* species (Basavanapada)	*Chadrunshi. Bauhinia.*	A small tree of no value.
37	*Bambusa bambos* (Dowga)	*Bamboos.*	Large, but not solid.
38	*Lagerstroemia parviflora* (Channangi)	*Chaningy. Lagerstroemia parviflora* Roxb.	
39	*Lannea coromandelica* (Godda)	*Goda.*	The *Amutty* of *Magadi.* Large and in plenty. Here its timber is reckoned to be bad.
40	An unidentified species	*Shilla.*	A large excellent timber-tree, of which I could get no specimen. It is quite different from the *Shalay* of *Magadi.*

Annexure - III

TREES OF THE CANARA FORESTS (NEAR *CADERI*) AS MENTIONED BY BUCHANAN

Buchanan has provided details of trees found in the forests of Canara (near *Caderi,* or Kadra) which he visited during March 5, 1801. The names of the trees as given by Buchanan and his comments are reproduced in the 3rd and 4th columns of the following table:

Sl. No.	Present scientific and local names	Local and scientific names used by Buchanan	Comments of Buchanan
(1)	(2)	(3)	(4)
1	*Bambusa bambos* (Dowga bamboo)	Prickly *Bamboo,* called *Colaki.*	The most common.
2	*Schleichera oleosa* (Kusum/ Sagadi)	*Cussum,* or *Shaguda* of my MSS.	Is very hard, and strong, and is used for the cylinders of sugar-mills.

3	*Terminalia paniculata* (hunal/huluve/kindal)	*Rindela, Chuncoa Huliva*, Buch. MSS.	Is used only for the beams of the houses of the natives.
4	*Holigarna grahamii* (Biba/Bipte/Biboi)	*Biba, Holigarna*, Buch: MSS.	This is the varnish tree of *Chittagong*, and I suppose of *Ava*. The natives here are only acquainted with the caustic nature of its juice, apply it to no use.
5	*Anthocephalus chinensis* (Kadamba/Apate)	*Cadumba*, the *Nauclea purpurea* Rox:	A large tree used for planks.
6	*Terminalia tomentosa* (Matti)	*Maratu*, a *Chuncoa* called by Dr. Roxburgh *Terminalia alata glubra*,	Grows to a very large size, and is used for building boats and canoes.
7	*Vitex trifolia* (Nochi)	*Beiladu, Vitex folis ternatis*,	Of hardly any use.
8	*Strychnos nux-vomica* (Kasarka)	*Cajeru, Strychnos Nux vomica*.	
9	*Adina cordifolia* (Heddi/Yethega)	*Hedu, Nauclea Daduga* Roxb: MSS,	A large tree fit for planks.
10	*Careya arborea* (Kaval/Kumbi)	*Cumbia*. The *Pelou* of the *Hort. Mal.*	

11	*Cinnamomum* species (Dalchinni)	*Ticay, Laurus Cassia.*	People from above the *Ghats* come to collect both the bark and the buds, which the natives call *Cabob-China.*
12	*Gardenia uliginosa* (Kare/Pandri)	*Paynra. Gardenia uliginosa* Willd:	Of no use.
13	An unidentified species	*Hodogus. Arbor foliis suboppositis, estipulaceis, ovalibus, integerrimis.*	The timber is said to be very strong and durable, and to resist the white ants, even when buried in the ground.
14	*Dalbergia latifolia* (Beete/Sissum)	*Sissa. Pterocarpus Sissoo* Roxb: MSS.	Is found in great plenty near the river toward the *Ghats.*
15	*Dillenia pentagyna* (Kanagal)	*Dillenia pentagyna* Roxb:	The natives have no name for it.
16	*Xylia xylocarpa* (Jamba)	*Jambay. Mimosa xylocarpon* Roxb.	It grows to an immense size.
17	*Bassia longifolia* (Ippe)	*Bassia longifolia.*	
18	*Pongamia pinnata* (Honge)	*Robinia mitis.*	
19	*Syzygium cumini* (Neral)	*Myrtus cumini.*	

TREES OF THE CANARA FORESTS (NEAR *CUTAKI*) AS MENTIONED BY BUCHANAN

Buchanan has provided details of trees found in the forests of Canara (near *Cutaki*, or *Kattige*) which he visited on March 9, 1801. The names of the trees as given by Buchanan and his comments are reproduced in the 3rd and 4th columns of the following table:

Sl. No.	Present scientific and local names	Local and scientific names used by Buchanan	Comments of Buchanan
1	*Terminalia bellirica* (Tari/ Ghoting)	*Tari, Myrobalanus Taria* Buch: MSS	
2	*Xylia xylocarpa* (Jamba)	*Jamba, Mimosa xylocarpon* Roxb:	
3	*Lagerstroemia lanceolata* (Nandi/ Nana)	*Nandy, foliis oppositis, non stipulaceis, integerrimis, subtus tomentosis.*	This is reckoned to make good planks and beams.

4	An unidentified species	*Unda Muraga, follis oppositis, integerrimis stipulis inter folia ut in Rubiaceis positis.*	Also reckoned good for planks and beams.
5	*Terminalia tomentosa* (Matti)	*Mutti, Chuncoa Muttia* Buch: MSS.	Good timber.
6	*Michelia champaka* (Sampige)	*Sampigy, Michelia Champaca.*	The wood used for drums.
7	*Schleichera oleosa* (Kusum/Sagadi)	*Shaguddy., Shaguda* Buch: MSS	A strong timber.
8	*Artocarpus lakucha* (Watehuli)	*Wontay. Artocarpus Bengalensis* Roxb: MSS.	The fruit is about the size of an orange, and is preserved with salt. Here it is used by the natives in place of tamarinds, which are much employed by the *Hindu* cooks.
9	*Pterocarpus marsupium* (Honne)	*Honnay. Pterocarpus santalinus* Willd:	

A SHORT BIOGRAPHY OF DR FRANCIS BUCHANAN

(Later known as Francis Hamilton or Francis Buchanan-Hamilton)

Francis Buchanan was born at the estate of Branziet, in Stirlingshire, Scotland, on the 15th of February, 1762. His father, Thomas Buchanan, was a Doctor, and his mother Elizabeth Hamilton, was the heiress of Burdowie, near Glasgow. Francis Buchanan passed his matriculation in 1774 and received an MA in 1779. He studied medicine in the University of Edinburgh, receiving his MD in 1783. His thesis was on *Malaria*. He also studied botany concurrently in the University of Edinburgh under John Hope, who was among the first in Britain to teach the Linnaean system of botanical nomenclature.

Buchanan spent his early career as a medical officer with the East India Company, spending his time aboard the Company's ships plying in the Asian region. The first few years were spent aboard the *Duke of Montrose* sailing between Bombay and China. He then served on the *Phoenix* sailing along the Coromandel Coast. In 1794, he served on the *Rose*, sailing from Portsmouth to Calcutta, reaching Calcutta in September. He then joined the Medical Service of the Bengal Presidency.

Immediately after his appointment as Assistant Surgeon, Buchanan proceeded to the Kingdom of Ava in Burma for a political mission under Captain Symes. The Ava mission, set sail on the *Sea Horse*, enabled Buchanan to undertake extensive botanical explorations in the Andaman Islands, Pegu (southern Myanmar), and Ava (northern Myanmar). On his return from this mission, Buchanan was stationed at Luckipore (Lakshmipur – now in Bangladesh), in the mouth of the river Brahmaputra (Meghna), where he wrote an admirable description of the fishes of the river. At the recommendation of Dr. William Roxburgh, then Superintendent of the Botanical Garden, Calcutta, he was employed by the Board of Trade at Calcutta to proceed to Chittagong and its vicinity, part of the ancient Kingdom of Tripura, which opened a wide field for his botanical and zoological explorations. Buchanan's narrations were eventually published in the book *Francis Buchanan in Southeast Bengal (1798)*.

In 1800, after the defeat of Tipu Sultan and the fall of the Mysore Kingdom, Buchanan was asked by the Governor-General of India, Lord Wellesley, to survey and report upon the conquered territories of Mysore, Malabar and Canara. Buchanan's long journey through these territories spanning more than fourteen months resulted in the publication of *A Journey from Madras through the Countries of Mysore, Canara and Malabar* (1807) in three volumes. In 1802, Buchanan was nominated to accompany the Embassy under Captain Knox to the Kingdom of Nepal. He stayed in Nepal for about fourteen months, which helped him in making large additions to the collection of rare plants, and in accumulating materials for his History of Nepal. On his return from Nepal, Buchanan was appointed Surgeon to the Governor-General of India, at Calcutta. During this period, he managed a menagerie which later became the Calcutta Alipore Zoo. In 1804, he was in charge of the Institution for Promoting the Natural History of India founded by Wellesley at Barrackpore. In 1806, he accompanied Lord Wellesley to England. However, his stay in England was not for many months, as he was again sent out to India to make a statistical survey of the Presidency of Bengal. However, this prodigious undertaking did not cover all the areas of the Presidency when it was closed prematurely in 1814. From 1807 to 1814, Buchanan had surveyed only portion of the territories, namely, the districts of Bihar and Patna, Shahabad, Bhagalpur, Dinajpur, Purnia, Rangpur, and Assam, covering more than sixty thousand square miles, and fifteen millions of people. Buchanan's reports and the materials collected by him were forwarded by the Government of Bengal to the Home Authorities in 1816, and were deposited in the East-India House. [Soon after Buchanan's death, his reports were edited and published by R. Montgomery Martin as *The History, Antiquities, Topography, and Statistics of Eastern India*. The book *Journal of Francis Buchanan kept during the survey of the districts of Patna and Gaya in 1811-12* was published in 1925 with an introduction by V. H. Jackson.]

Buchanan succeeded Dr. William Roxburgh to become the Superintendent of the Calcutta Botanical Garden in 1814, but was compelled to return to Britain in the following year due to his ill health. On his arrival in England, he presented his large and fine collection of plants, animals, coins, MSS., etc. to the Court of Directors. Buchanan had also collected a series of watercolors of Indian and Nepalese plants and animals, probably painted by Indian artists, which are now in the library of the Linnaean Society of London. In 1818, he changed his name to Francis Hamilton after inheriting the estate of his mother. However, he continued to be variously referred to by others as Buchanan-Hamilton, Francis Hamilton Buchanan, or Francis Buchanan Hamilton. He fixed his residence at Leney, in Perthshire, Scotland, and devoted himself to completing his natural history manuscripts. He also contributed largely to various literary and scientific societies. He was elected Fellow of Royal Society, London and Edinburgh, Member of Royal Asiatic Society, etc. In 1819, he published *An Account of the Kingdom of Nepal*, based on his observations during the period 1802-03 and information obtained from various sources in the subsequent years. During the same year, he published his *Genealogies of the Hindus, Extracted from their Sacred Writings*. In 1822, he published *An account of the fishes found in the river Ganges and its branches*, which describes over 100 species not formerly recognized scientifically.

Buchanan married late in his life, had a son, and died on the 15th of June, 1829, in the 67th year of his age. The tree (genus) *Buchanania* was named in honor of Francis Buchanan. A species of South Asian turtle, *Geoclemys hamiltonii* (black pond turtle/spotted pond turtle) was named to commemorate him. The fish *Thryssa hamiltonii* is one of the many fish named after Hamilton.

AN INTERESTING 'LOST AND FOUND' CASE

During a voyage in 1785, Francis Buchanan had lent to his shipmate, Alexander Boswell, the notes that he had taken of John Hope's botany lectures in the University of Edinburgh while he was a student. Unfortunately, Boswell lost the notes in Satyamangala, then in the Mysore Kingdom. Somehow, the notes went into the hands of the ruler of Mysore, Tipu Sultan, who had them rebound. In 1800, after the fall of Mysore, they were found in Tipu's library at Srirangapatna by a British major who returned them to Buchanan.

[**Source**: en.m.wikipedia.org]